Braid

COMPLETE BOOK of FISHING SYSTEMS

by Geoff Wilson

COMPLETE BOOK of FISHING SYSTEMS

by Geoff Wilson

All Diagrams, Artwork & Text
GEOFF WILSON

Editor & Consultant
BILL CLASSON

Design & Production
AUSTRALIAN FISHING NETWORK

AFN
AUSTRALIAN FISHING NETWORK

First published in 2011
by Australian Fishing Network
PO Box 544, Croydon, VIC 3136
Telephone: +61 3 9729 8788
Facsimile: +61 3 9729 7833
Email: sales@afn.com.au
Website: www.afn.com.au

USA Bookseller: Cardinal Publishers Group
7301 Georgetown Road, Suite 118 Indianapolis, IN 46268
Voice: (317) 879 0871 Facsimile: (317) 879 0872
Toll Free: (800) 296 0281
Website: www.cardinalpub.com

ISBN 9781 8651 3185 6

Printed in China

Foreword

The most expensive car on the road is a liability with bald tyres because the tyres on your car provide its connection with the road. Likewise the most expensive tackle is of little use if your connection to the fish is suspect.

Unfortunately, there are too many cars on the road with bald tyres, just as there are far too many anglers whose otherwise sound equipment is compromised by their connection to a good fish with unsound and poorly tied rigs.

In my previous publications of knots and rigs, I have compiled and illustrated a good many knots and rigs, from simple to more complex, more or less at random, simply because I could include more samples of each that way.

However, this publication progresses from tying various knots to their use in assembling suitable rigs to accommodate the required components such as the hook or hooks, sinker and swivel, float etc. For this reason there are fewer samples, but these are all that 90% of anglers will need.

I have not included the supposed percentages of the line's breaking strain that these knots retain. These are misleading because the strength of a knot will vary depending on things like how well the knot was tied, and whether the knot has been re-tied since the last trip, or maybe the one before.

In addition, the compatibility of components like the diameter of the line versus the diameter of the metal from which the hook (or ring, or swivel) was drawn will affect the percentage of the line's breaking strain at which a knot will fail.

Knots may not be as sexy a say a finely engineered reel, or perhaps a rod made from the most technologically advanced components. However, should your reel fail, and you have to handline a fish, as I have done on occasion: Or should your rod break, which is by no means unheard of, you may still retrieve your catch. But if your knot fails, forget it.

About the Author

Geoff Wilson had an obsession with fishing from an early age and at around age 9, was presented with a book entitled "*Luron Fishing Lines for Angling*" by his Father Gordon. The book was a guide to the proper use of the new nylon monofilament fishing lines that were beginning to displace the cat-gut and cotton lines and was published in 1951 by Imperial Chemical Industries Ltd,. Plastics Division, Welwyn Garden City, Hertfordshire, England.

Of particular interest were the knot illustrations by noted angler and illustrator Alex Jardine. Geoff studied those illustrations and became proficient in the tying of those illustrated knots, much more so that many more mature anglers who struggled with this aspect of fishing. This, in turn lead to Geoff illustrating his own book of *Fishing Knots and Rigs* back in 1990, the ongoing sales of which have identified an ongoing need for publications such as this.

CONTENTS

Chapter 1

THE UNI KNOT

Rigging with the Uni Knot

There are several variations of the Uni Knot but the one described is the easiest to tie and the most useful.

The Uni knot is a sliding noose that tightens on the eye of the hook, lure, ring or swivel. Its great advantage is that it can be tied in lines both heavy and light and provides adequate strength for most situations.

Tying on a hook using the Uni Knot

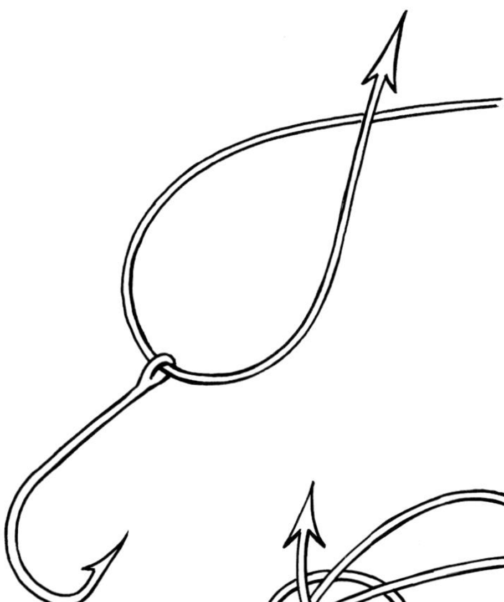

1. Thread the eye of the hook then pull sufficient line through to encircle the source line with the tag.

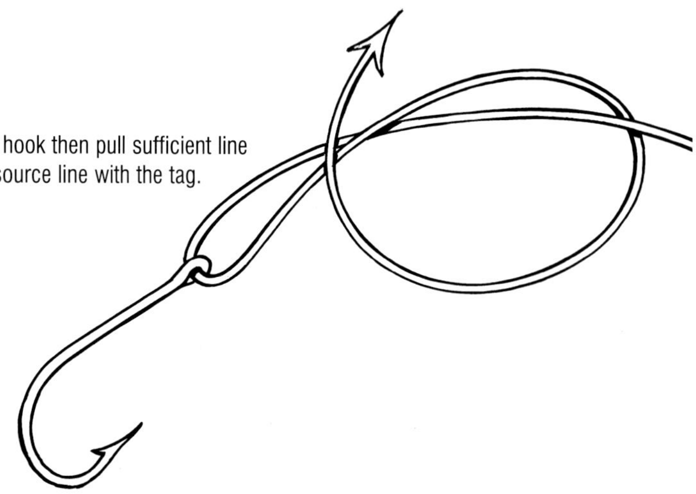

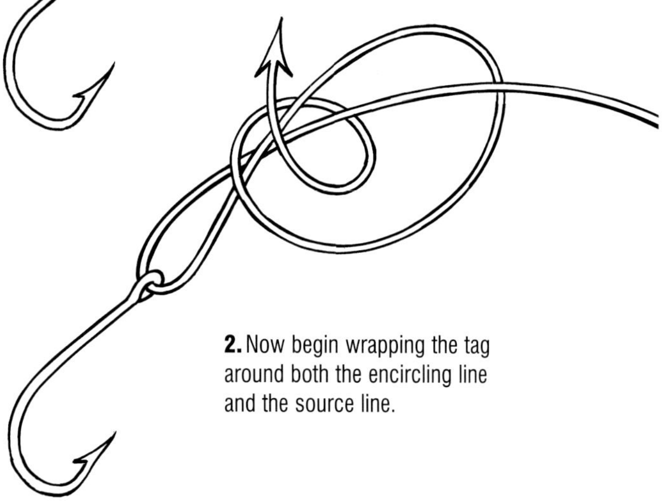

2. Now begin wrapping the tag around both the encircling line and the source line.

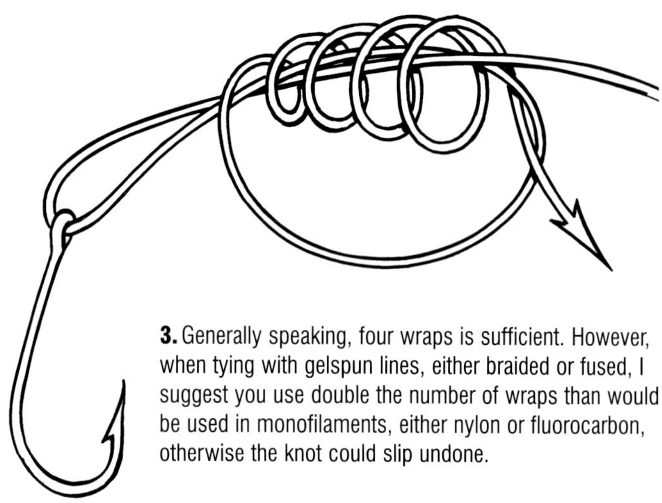

3. Generally speaking, four wraps is sufficient. However, when tying with gelspun lines, either braided or fused, I suggest you use double the number of wraps than would be used in monofilaments, either nylon or fluorocarbon, otherwise the knot could slip undone.

4. Close the knot.

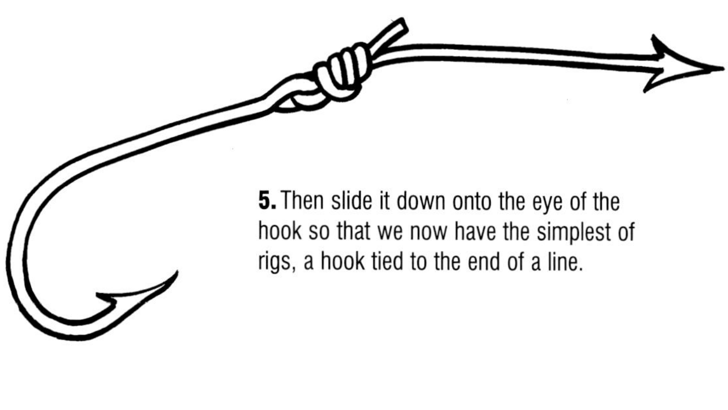

5. Then slide it down onto the eye of the hook so that we now have the simplest of rigs, a hook tied to the end of a line.

Rigging a Simple Running Sinker using a Uni Knot

Because an unweighted bait has limited application and is restricted by the depth of water, the inability to cast it very far, and other factors like wind and current, a small sinker may be required.

1. Sliding a small ball, bean or barrel sinker, onto the line before attaching the hook allows you to make ...

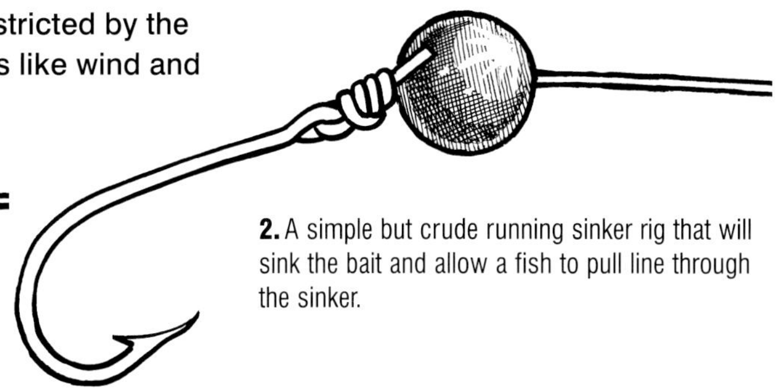

2. A simple but crude running sinker rig that will sink the bait and allow a fish to pull line through the sinker.

Making a Trace using a Uni Knot

1. Shown is the construction of a simple monofilament trace that can be from say, 12 inches (30 cm) to 3 feet (90 cm) making use of a Uni Knot to tie a hook to one end and a swivel or solid metal ring to the other.

The really good thing about having a separate trace is that it can be of heavier line to give added protection when you have a large fish on that may wear through your lighter main line.

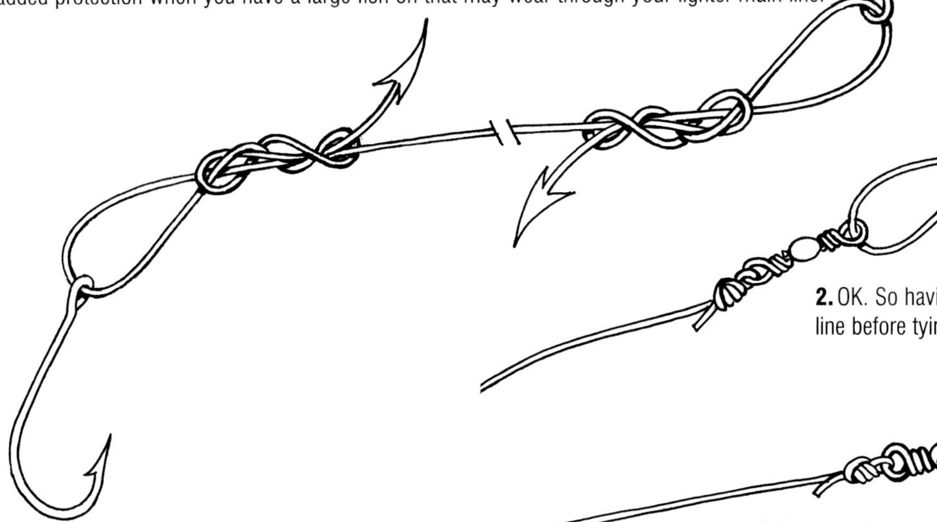

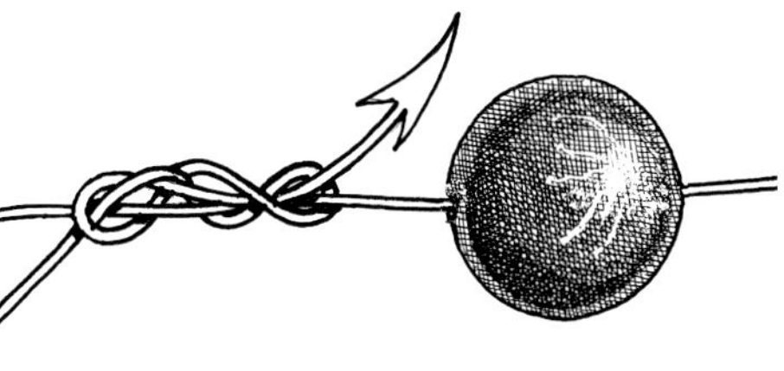

2. OK. So having made your trace, thread a sinker onto the main line before tying it to the swivel or ring on your trace.

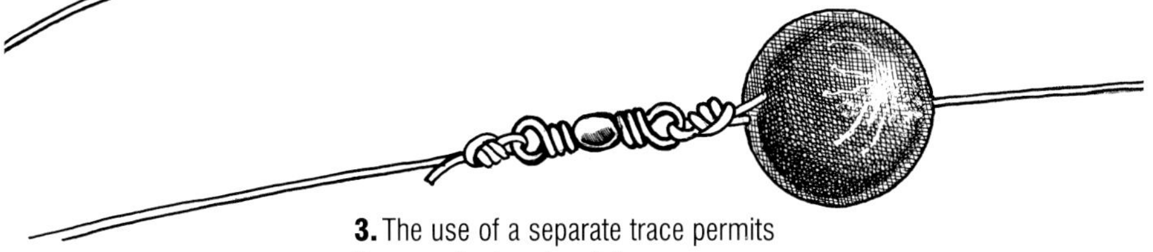

3. The use of a separate trace permits the use of a heavier sinker.

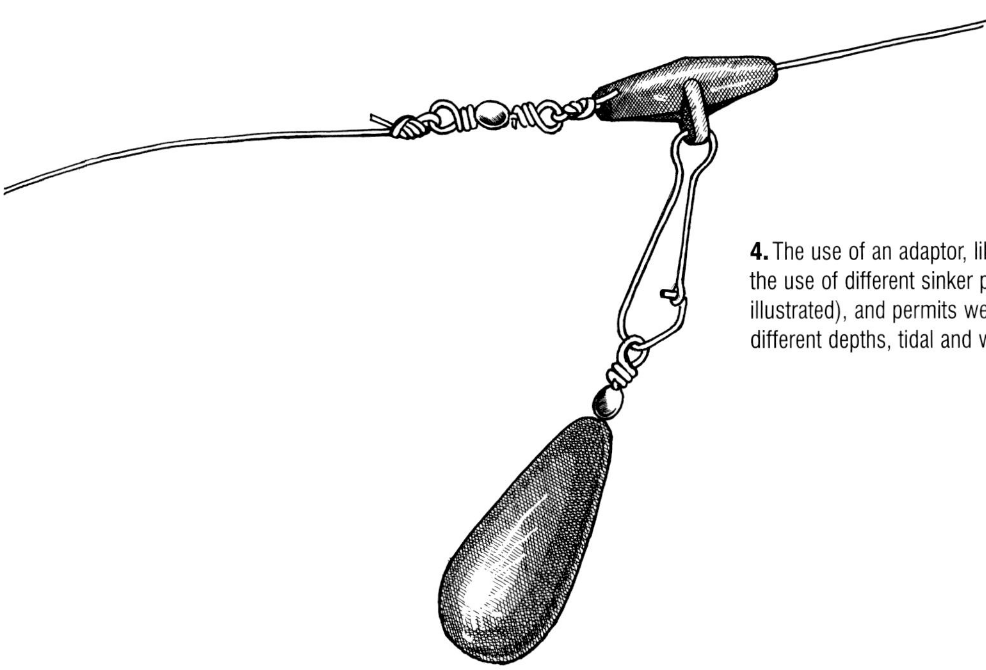

4. The use of an adaptor, like the Ezy Rig (illustrated) permits the use of different sinker patterns like the bomb (also illustrated), and permits weights to be changed to hold in different depths, tidal and wind conditions.

Attaching your line to a reel using the Uni Knot

Using a Uni Knot to attach new line to your reel is dead easy.

When attaching gelspun lines, either braided or fused, it is advisable to make several additional wraps around the spool, and – when using gelspun lines on game fishing tackle – wrapping a small amount of adhesive electrician's tape around the bare spool arbour before winding the line on will prevent the line from revolving on the spool with the application of heavy drag settings.

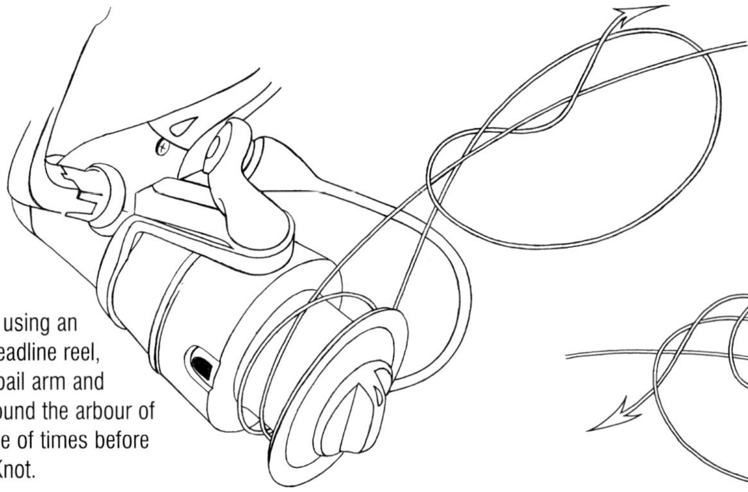

1. Should you be using an egg-beater or threadline reel, simply open the bail arm and wrap the loop around the arbour of the spool a couple of times before forming the Uni Knot.

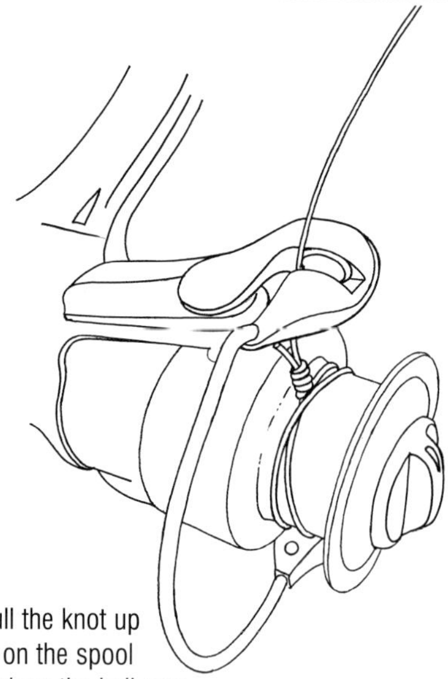

2. Pull the knot up tight on the spool and close the bail arm.

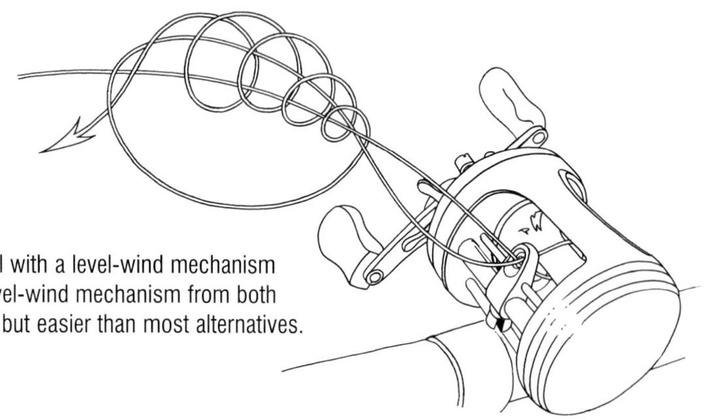

3. Naturally, when using a reel with a level-wind mechanism you will have to thread the level-wind mechanism from both directions, which is awkward but easier than most alternatives.

Joining lines using the double Uni Knot

The Double Uni Knot is used for joining two monofilament lines of similar or different diameters. It is also used for joining gelspun lines, both braided and fused, albeit with a marked reduction in strength.

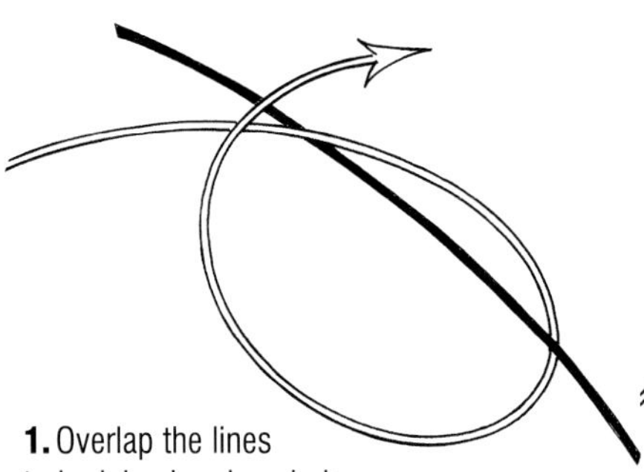

1. Overlap the lines to be joined and encircle one with the tag of the other.

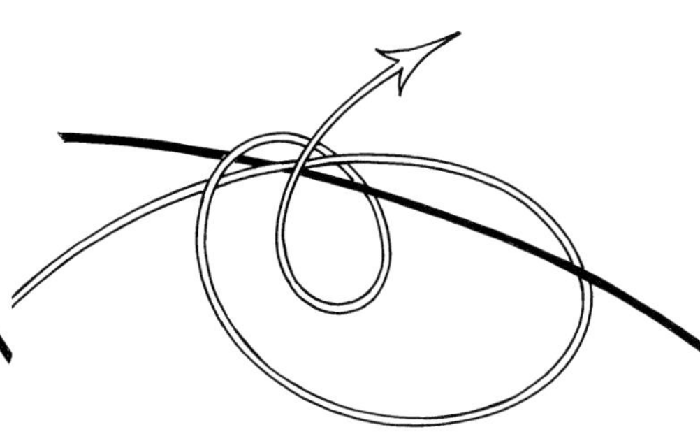

2. Begin wrapping both lines with the tag of the encircling line, working entirely inside the loop.

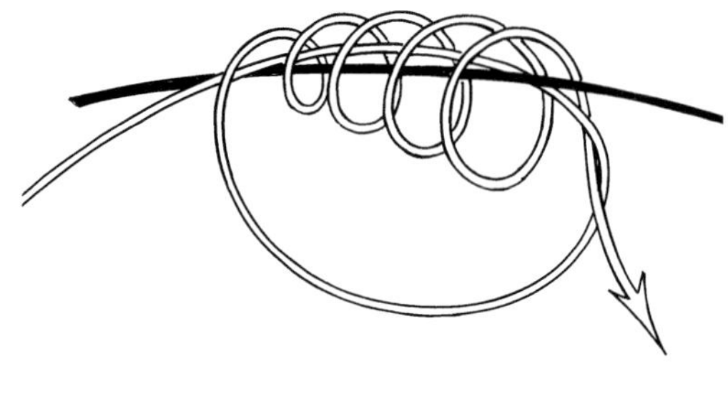

3. Four wraps is usually sufficient to ensure the Uni Knot won't slip. However, you may need to double that number when using gelspun lines, either braided or fused, and reduce the number of wraps to just three when tying it with a stiff or heavy line.

4. Close the knot but don't pull it really tight just yet. Then make the same configuration with the other line.

5. Close the second knot as you did the first.

6. Slide both knots together, pull each tight in turn then trim the tags.

Making a fixed loop using the Uni Knot

Lures, when rigged on heavy fluorocarbon or nylon monofilament leaders, are best attached with a loop that allows the lure more freedom to swim than if that heavy monofilament were tied directly to the towing eye of the lure. Shown is an example of making such a loop with a Uni Knot.

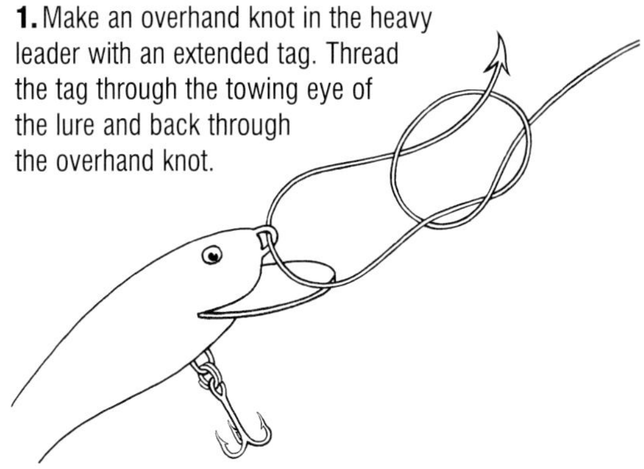

1. Make an overhand knot in the heavy leader with an extended tag. Thread the tag through the towing eye of the lure and back through the overhand knot.

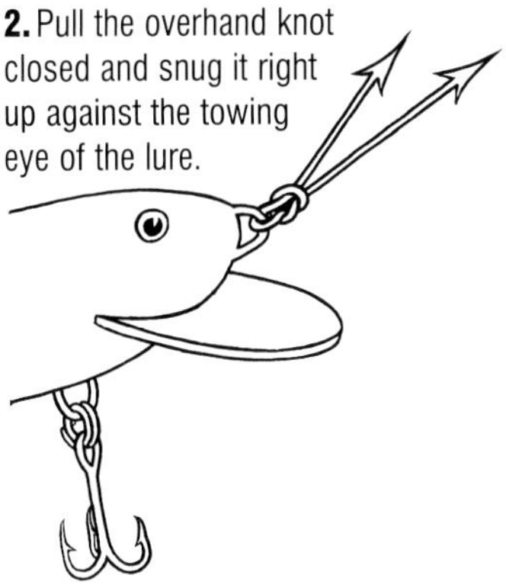

2. Pull the overhand knot closed and snug it right up against the towing eye of the lure.

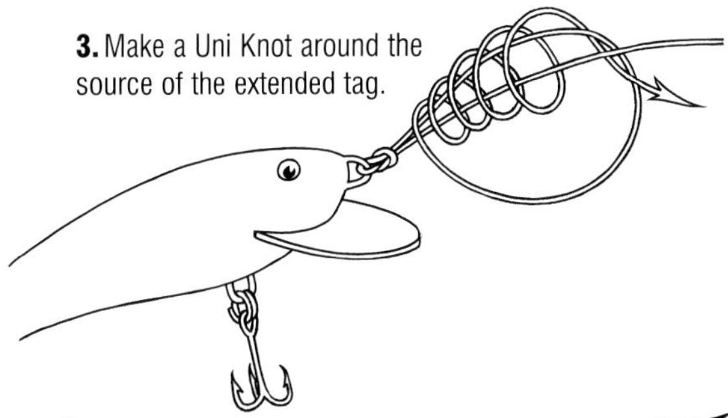

3. Make a Uni Knot around the source of the extended tag.

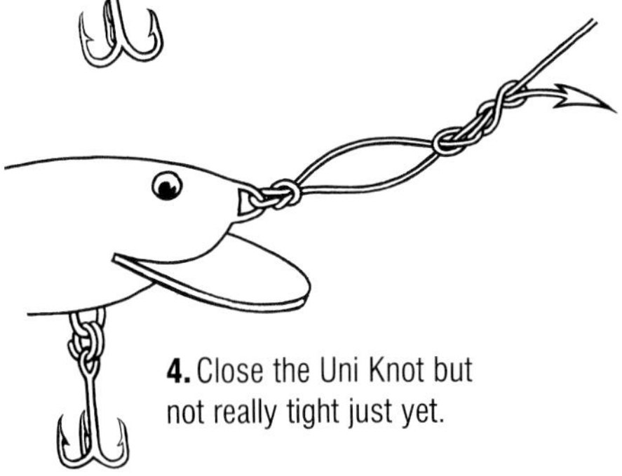

4. Close the Uni Knot but not really tight just yet.

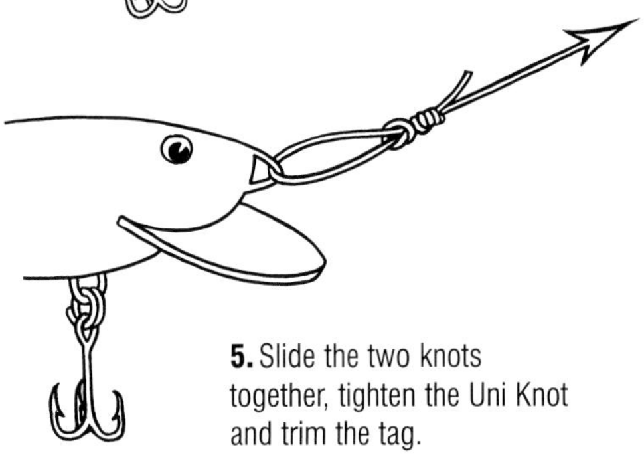

5. Slide the two knots together, tighten the Uni Knot and trim the tag.

This procedure is for attaching action lures to heavy monofilament leaders. Unfortunately many lures are lost because some folk use a loop to attach lures to really light lines or traces and the swimming motion of the lures just wears the loop through. When using light lines or traces, my advice is to either tie the line directly onto the towing eye, or attach the lure using a small metal clip.

Drop-shotting with the Uni Knot

Drop Shotting refers to the presentation of a hook or lure, not at the end of a line, but standing out from a line to which a sinker has been attached. This is a popular and effective rig when used in conjunction with soft plastics.

For each rig you will need a suitable, straight hook with a large eye, two small plastic beads, a soft plastic lure body and another length of line, usually 3 to 6 feet (to 2 metres) in length, to which your sinker is attached. This is referred to as the sinker length.

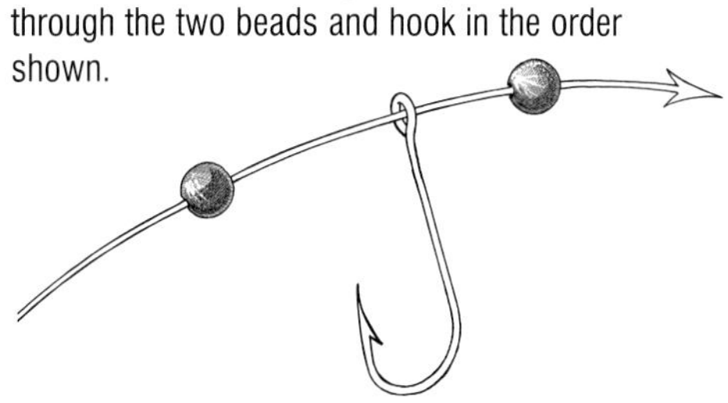

1. Thread the line coming from your rod and reel through the two beads and hook in the order shown.

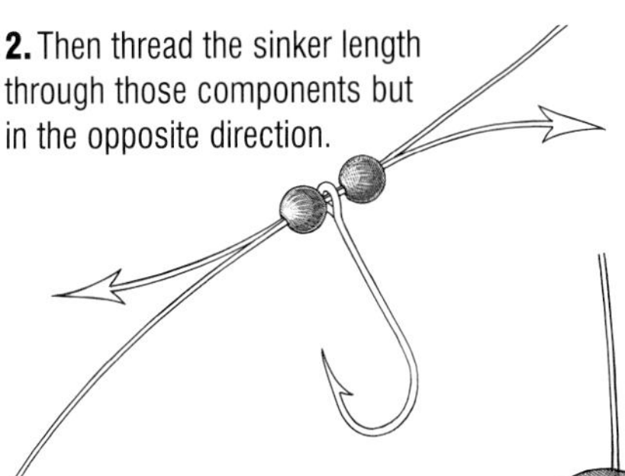

2. Then thread the sinker length through those components but in the opposite direction.

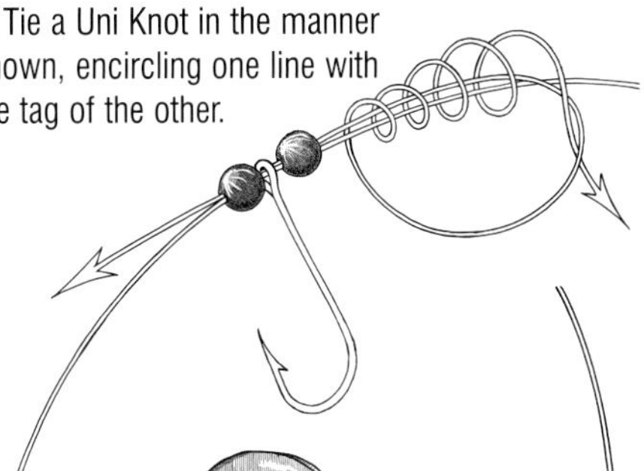

3. Tie a Uni Knot in the manner shown, encircling one line with the tag of the other.

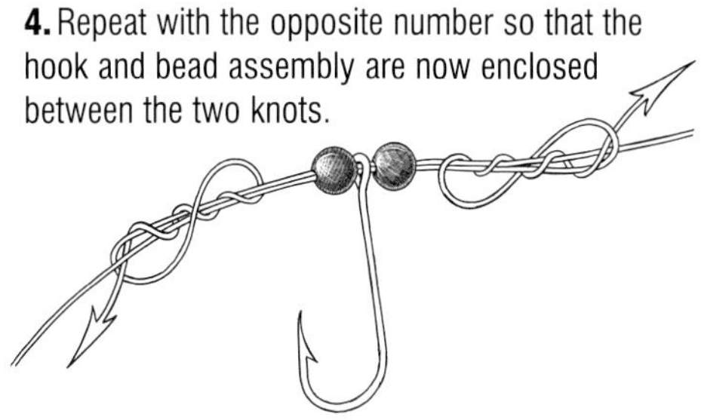

4. Repeat with the opposite number so that the hook and bead assembly are now enclosed between the two knots.

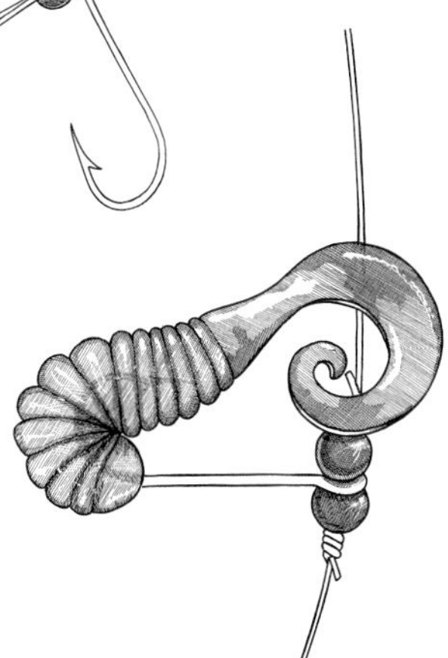

5. Close both Uni Knots, slide them together, and thread on your chosen soft plastic body.

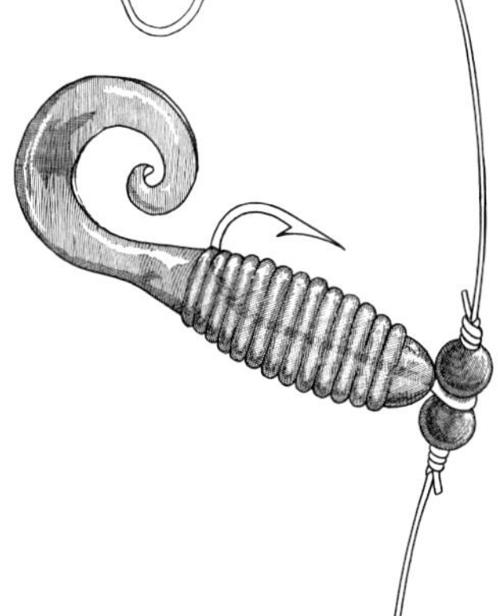

6. Shown is the finished presentation.

Chapter 2

BLOOD KNOT

Simple Rigging with the Blood Knot

Like the Uni Knot previously described, the Blood Knot may be used for tying on hooks, rings, and swivels. Although it is slightly more difficult to tie than a Uni Knot it provides a very strong connection.

There are several variations of the Blood Knot but the one described for tying on hooks is the strongest. That's provided the components: Line hook, swivel etc, are new, or at least clean, so that the line can be tightened without impediment.

Other examples of blood knots shown here include the Double Blood Knot for joining monofilament lines of similar diameter, the Twisted Dropper Loop, and the Blood Bight Loop which is used for attaching sinkers.

Tying on a hook using the Blood Knot

1. Thread the eye of the hook twice so that the illustrated configuration is formed.

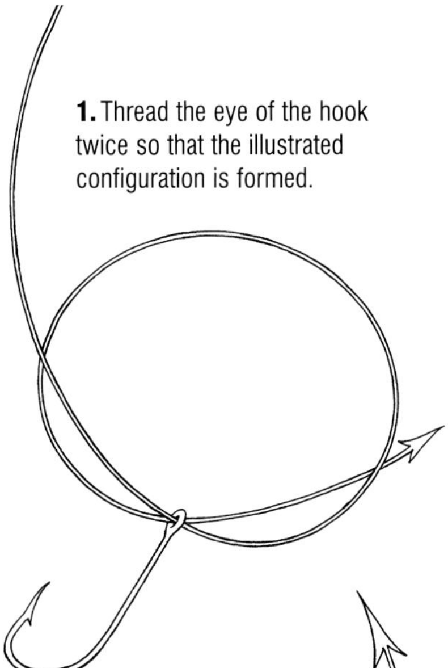

2. Having made a the double loop configuration on the eye of the hook ring or swivel, wind the tag back around the main or standing part of the line from three to six times; more wraps for lighter line, less for heavier line.

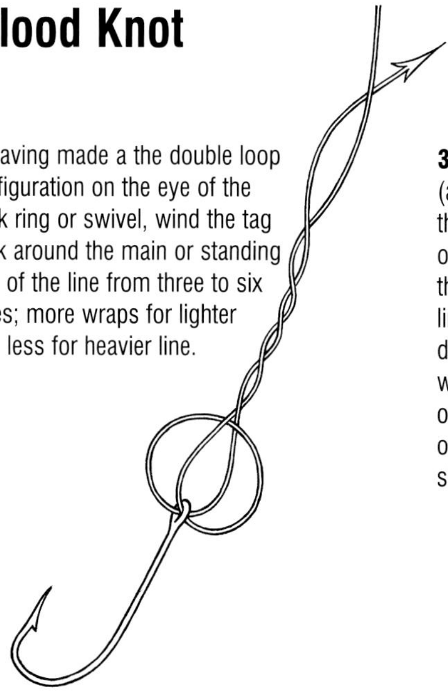

3. Generally speaking, four wraps (as shown here) are sufficient before threading the tag back through the original double loop configuration on the eye of the hook. However, gelspun lines, either braided or fused, require double the number of wraps than would be used in either nylon or fluorocarbon monofilaments, otherwise the knot could slip undone.

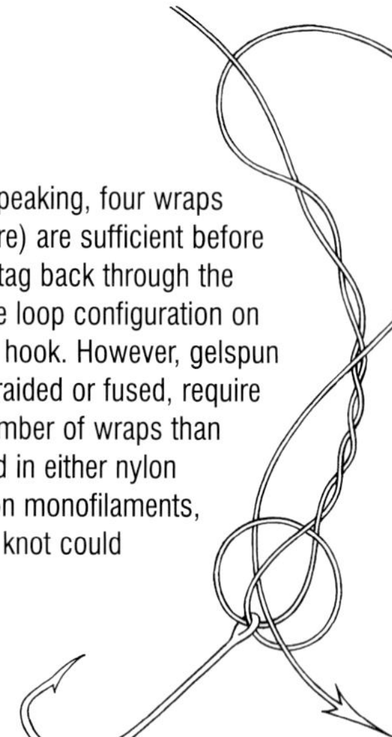

4. Close the knot pulling on the main line against, in this case, the hook.

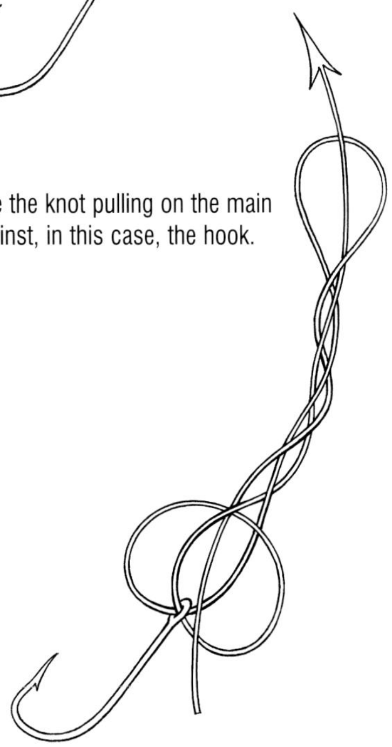

5. When the knot settles firmly on the eye, trim the tag and the connection is complete.

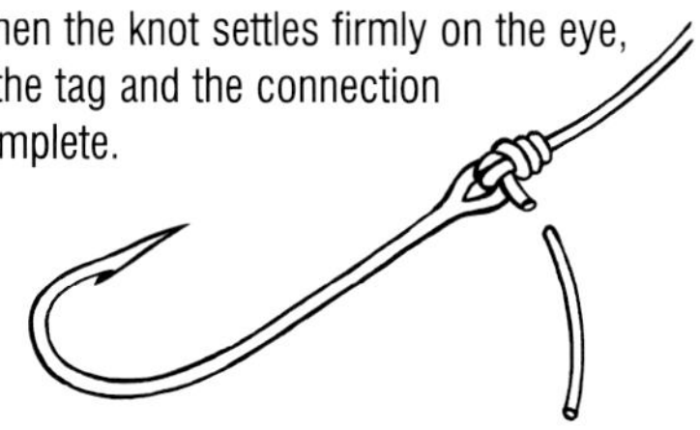

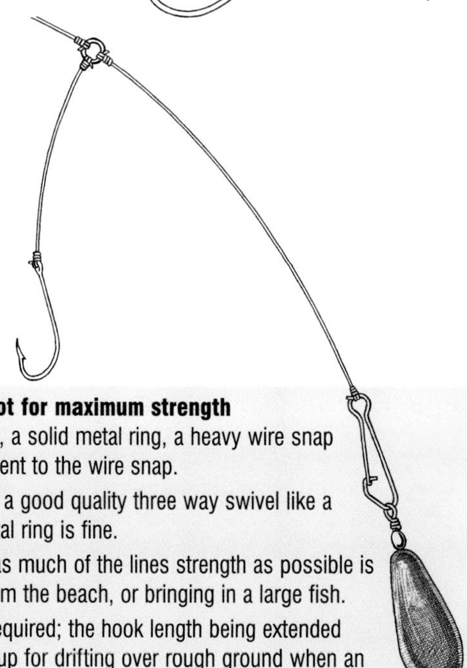

(6). Rigging with fixed sinker and Blood Knot for maximum strength

The components used with this rig are: The line, a solid metal ring, a heavy wire snap and a sinker with an eye that allows its attachment to the wire snap.

Of course you could replace the metal ring with a good quality three way swivel like a Spro, but for strength and simplicity a solid metal ring is fine.

Using the Blood Knot as described will ensure as much of the lines strength as possible is retained, minimising snap-offs when casting from the beach, or bringing in a large fish.

The hook and sinker lengths can be varied as required; the hook length being extended for fishing at anchor in fast tides, or shortened up for drifting over rough ground when an extended hook length would contribute to snagging.

Twisted Dropper Loop

Also included in the family of Blood Knots are the Dropper loop and Twisted Dropper loop. The only difference between then is that in the Twisted Dropper Loop, the one I have illustrated here, is that the line forming the loop is twisted into a spiral before being secured with the Blood Knot.

This configuration is used when tying up monofilament rigs of at least twice the breaking strain of the main line they are to be used with.

When rigging with the same strength line as the main line, use the rig previously described as "Rigging with fixed sinker and Blood Knot for maximum strength."

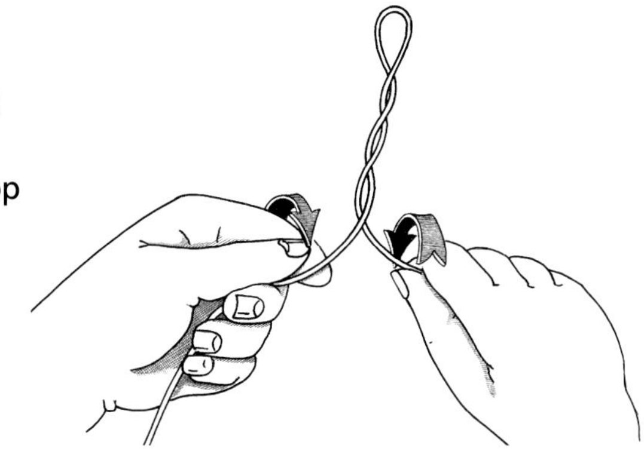

1. Twist the line where you want the hook to go, causing a loop to spiral out roughly at right angles to the main line.

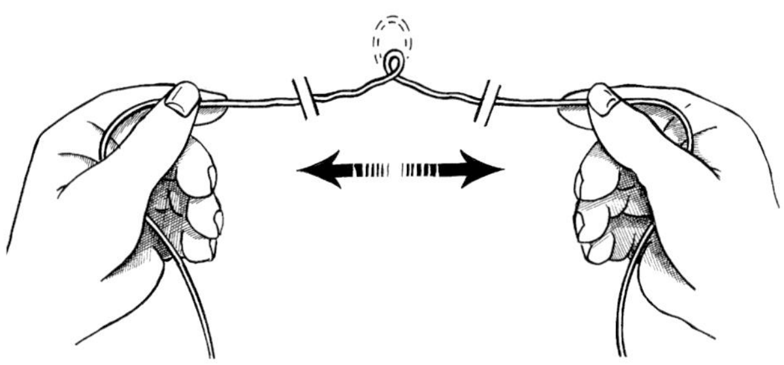

2. Having made a dozen or so twists, pull the spiral apart so that the loop size is reduced to pass more easily through the eye of the hook.

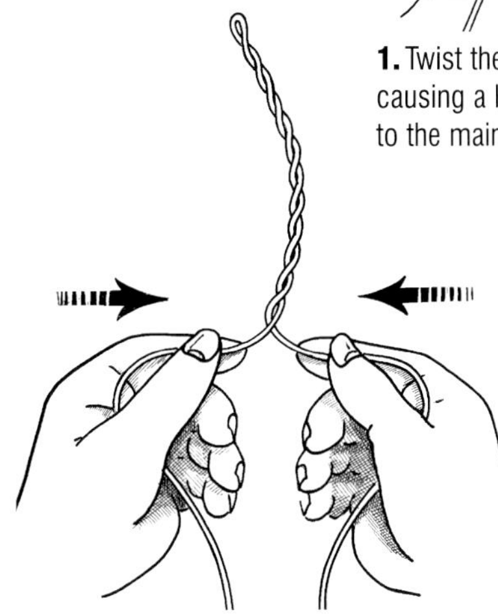

3. Allow the loop to spiral back under some tension so that the spiral is now slightly more compressed.

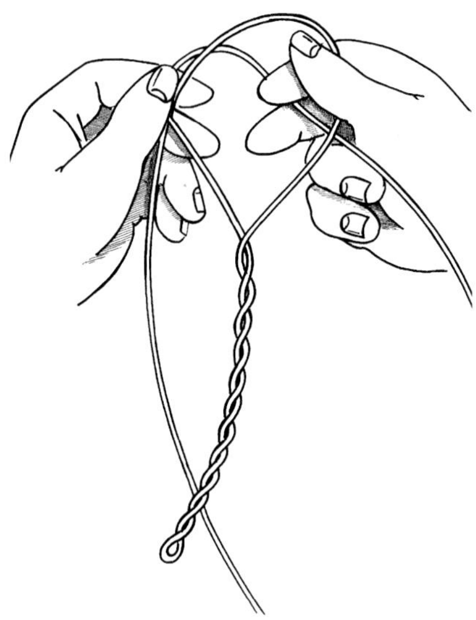

4. Isolate the spiral by crossing the line to form a loop. Your index finger goes between loop and tag to facilitate the rotation of the cross-over.

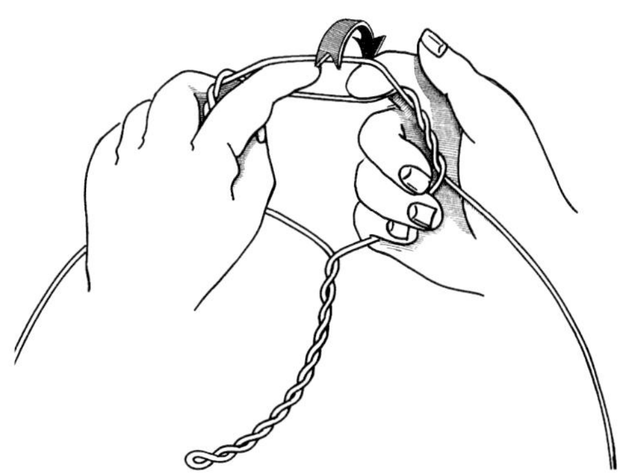

5. Twist the cross-over alternately, inserting then withdrawing the index finger of each hand as each half twist is added.

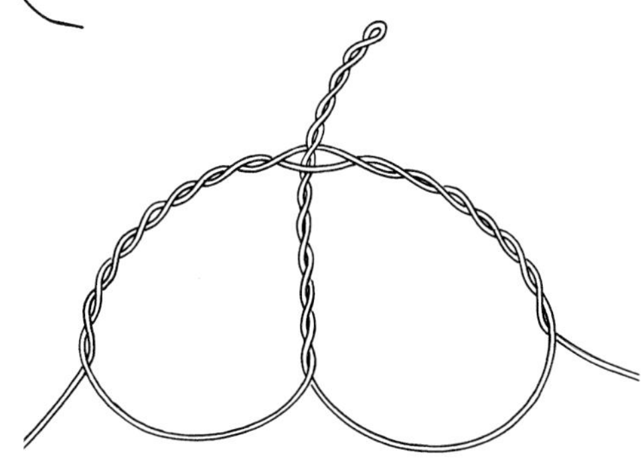

6. Having completed eight half twists, pass the spiral through the cross-over that you were rotating with your fingers.

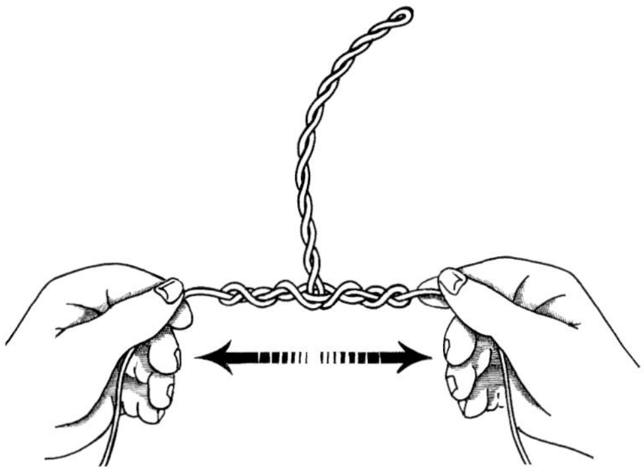

7. Close the knot with firm, even pressure.

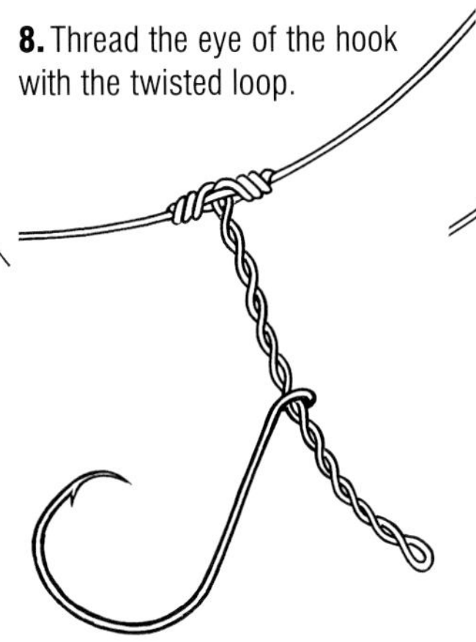

8. Thread the eye of the hook with the twisted loop.

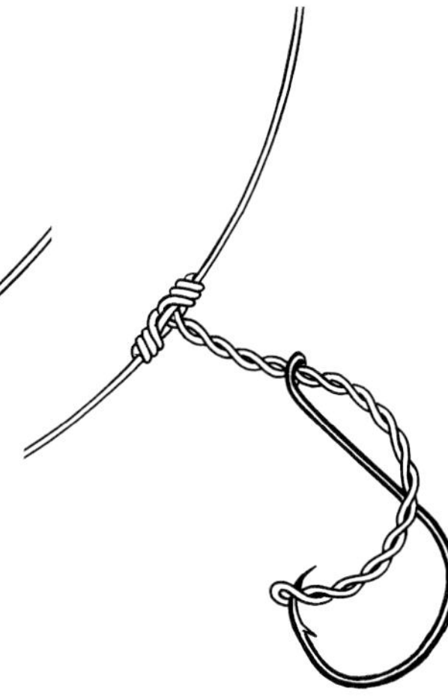

9. Then thread the point of the hook through the twisted loop.

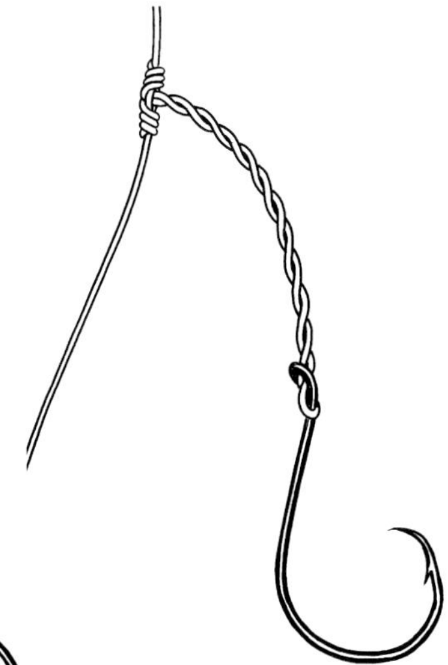

10. The hook is then presented far enough away from the line so that it is most unlikely to tangle.

Blood Bight Loop

The sinker is attached by tying a loop in the end of the line. In this case we use a Blood Bight (figure of eight) Loop.

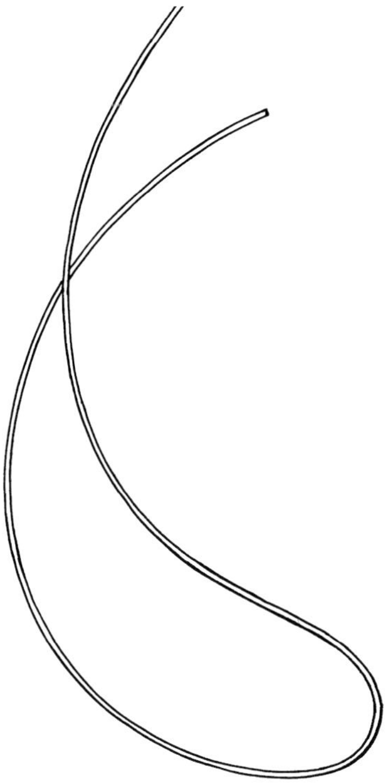

1. Make a loop in the end of the line.

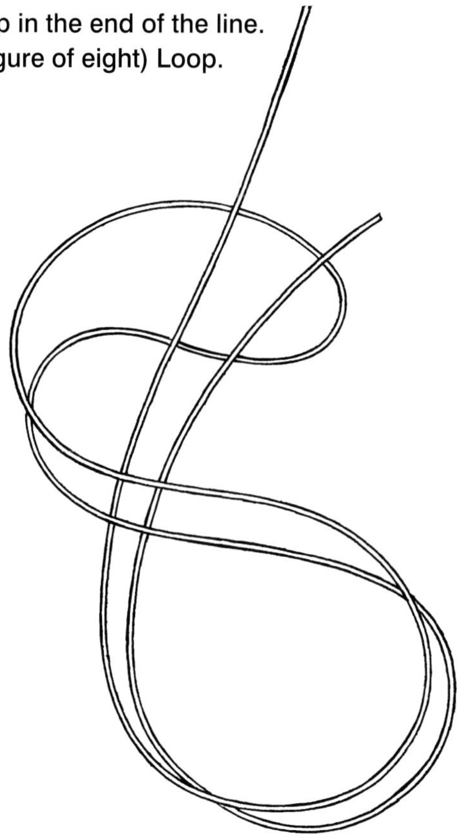

2. Wrap the loop back over itself as shown.

3. Then pass the loop through the bottom loop in the figure of eight to finish it off.

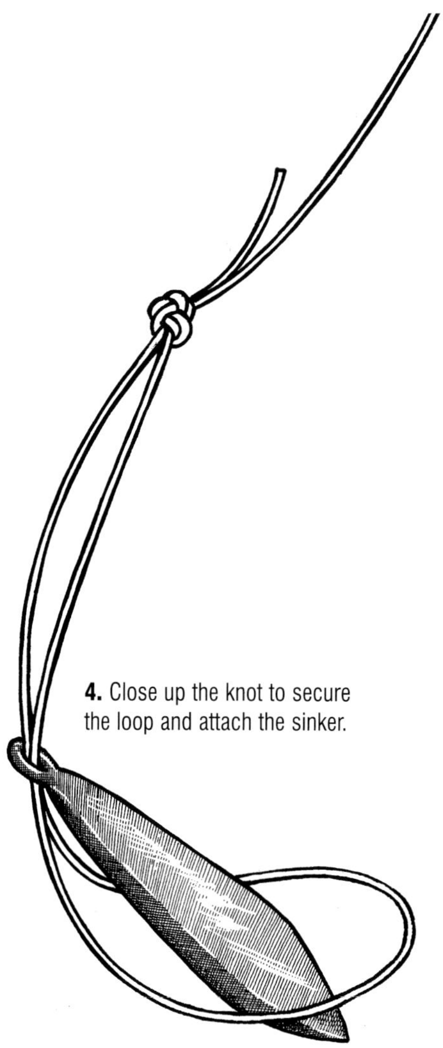

4. Close up the knot to secure the loop and attach the sinker.

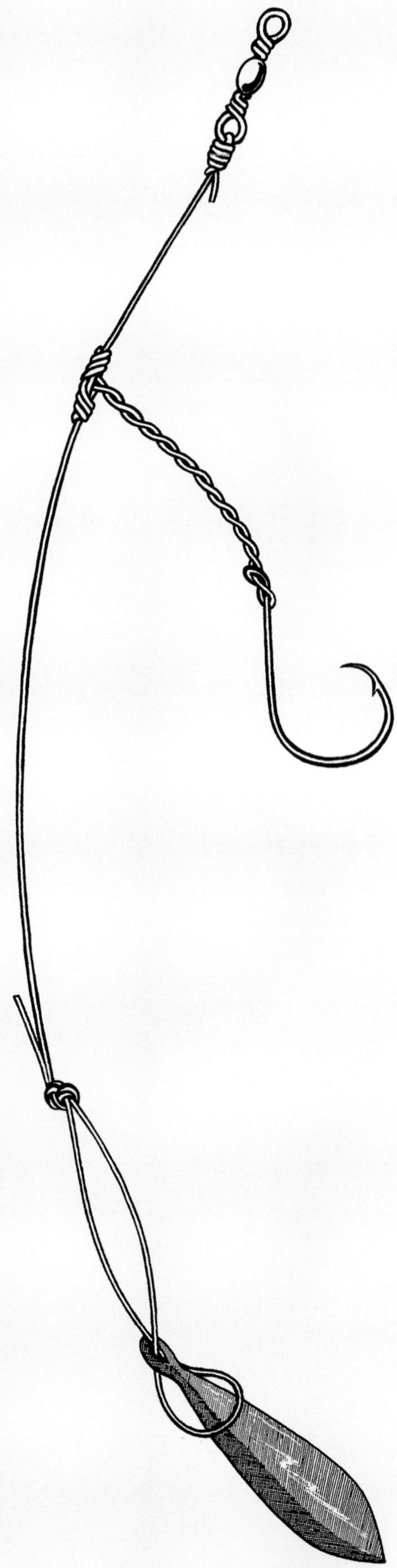

5. After attaching a swivel or solid metal ring to the top, using either the Uni Knot or Blood Knot, the rig is complete. Tie it onto you line, bait it up and you are ready to fish.

Joining lines of similar diameter using the Double Blood Knot

The Double Blood Knot shown is the neatest way of joining two similar monofilament fishing lines, providing adequate strength for most types of fishing. However, this join is not recommended for joining gelspun lines.

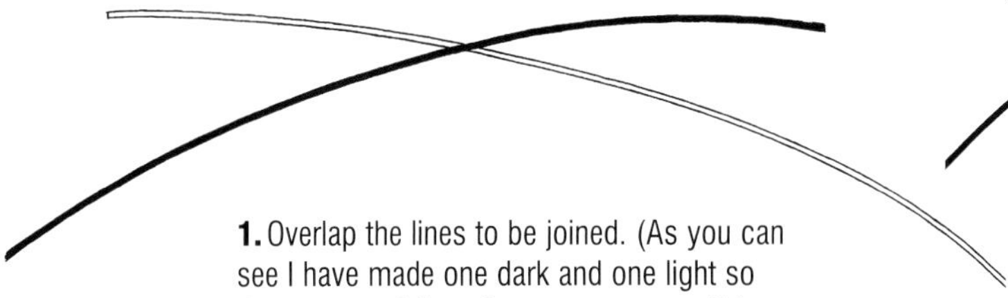

1. Overlap the lines to be joined. (As you can see I have made one dark and one light so that you can follow the steps more easily).

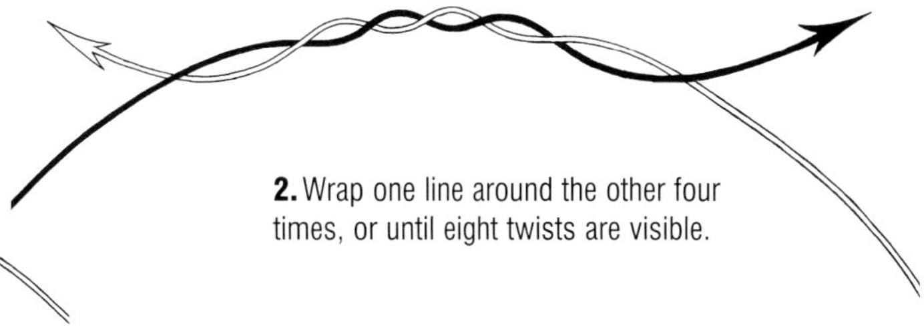

2. Wrap one line around the other four times, or until eight twists are visible.

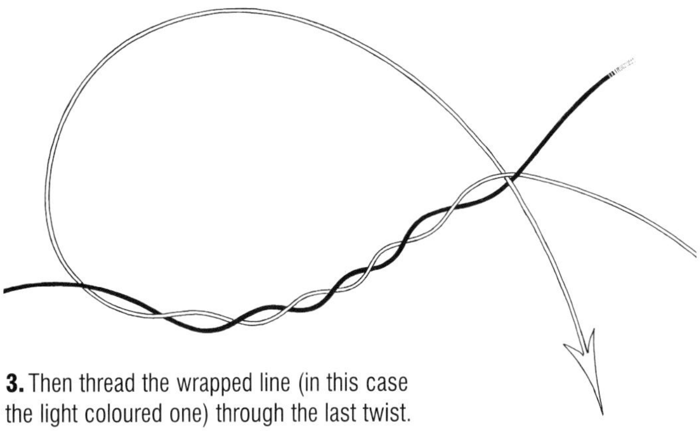

3. Then thread the wrapped line (in this case the light coloured one) through the last twist.

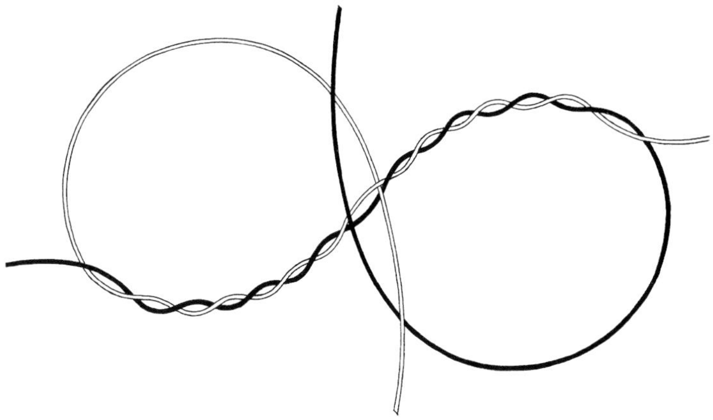

4. Continue the twisting process until the threaded twist is central, then thread the other (in this case the darker line) back though the central twist, only in the opposite direction to the other.

5. Close the knot by pulling the lines on each side until the knot begins to form.

6. When the knot is closed and tightened as far as it will go, trim the tags.

Chapter 3

TWISTED DROPPER LOOP

More on the Twisted Dropper Loop

We introduced the Twisted Dropper Loop in the previous chapter but we've not finished with it yet.

The following method of constructing a Twisted Dropper Loop can be used in either multi-strand wire or heavy monofilament and allows for the construction of much stronger rigs that are suitable for a range of presentations from deep sea fishing to surf casting.

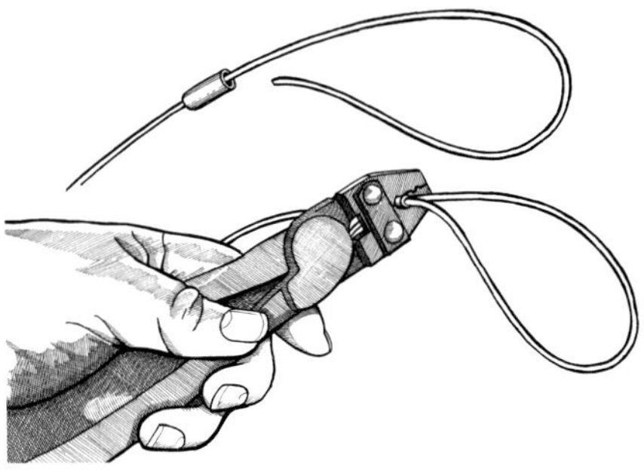

1. Take a 7 foot (2 metre) length of your heavy monofilament or multi-strand wire, either nylon coated or bare, and make a decent size loop in each end. You can tie the loop in monofilament, but I suggest you might like to secure the loops you made in the multi-strand wire with crimped sleeves.

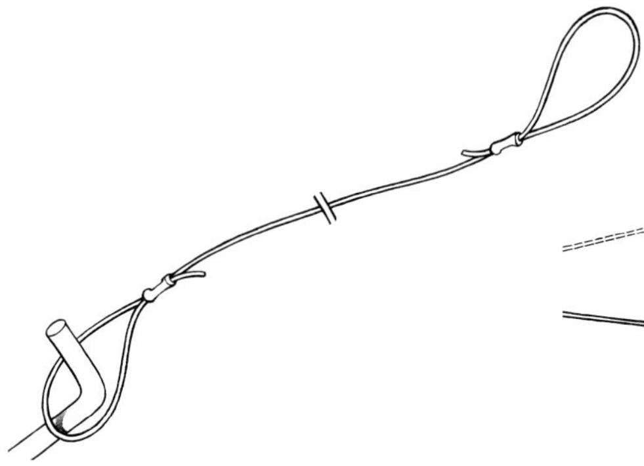

2. Place one of the loops over some fixed object, which could be a cleat or rod holder on your boat, clothesline handle or garden tap.

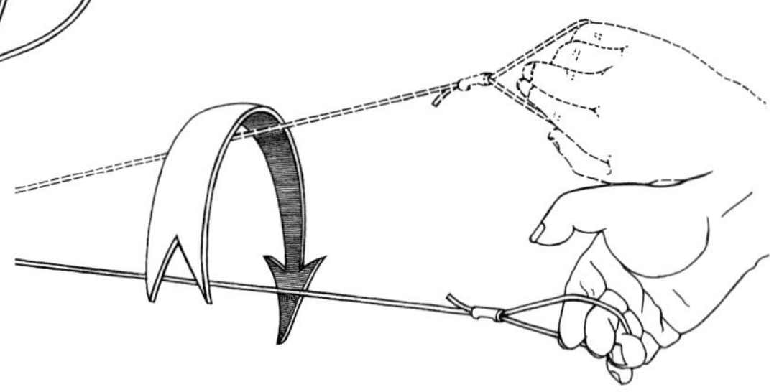

3. Then rotate the line about 100 times with your hand in the loop: Or – you could do as I do when I have a number to make up – and put an Allen key or the like, in the chuck of your drill and whiz it up on that. Don't overdo it though or you will end up with a mess.

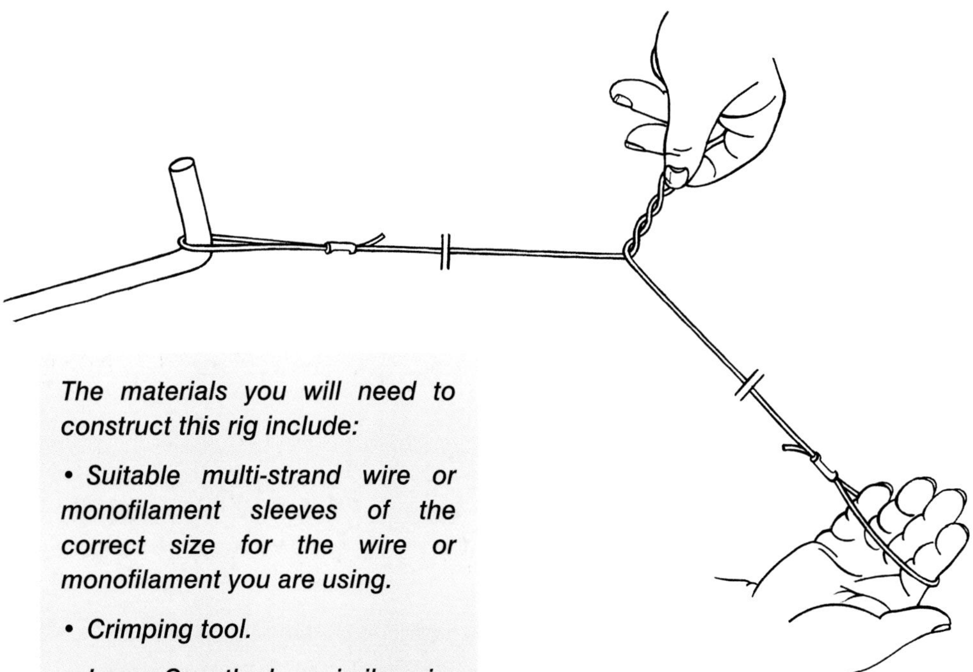

The materials you will need to construct this rig include:

- *Suitable multi-strand wire or monofilament sleeves of the correct size for the wire or monofilament you are using.*
- *Crimping tool.*
- *Large Coastlock or similar wire snap for attaching sinkers.*
- *Suitable size hooks for the size fish you are fishing for and the size of bait that you intend to use.*

4. Having twisted the line, hold it fairly tight. Then, with your finger, interrupt the twisted line in the middle to initiate a spiral loop; then allow the spiral loop to extend far enough out from the main line to put the hook on.

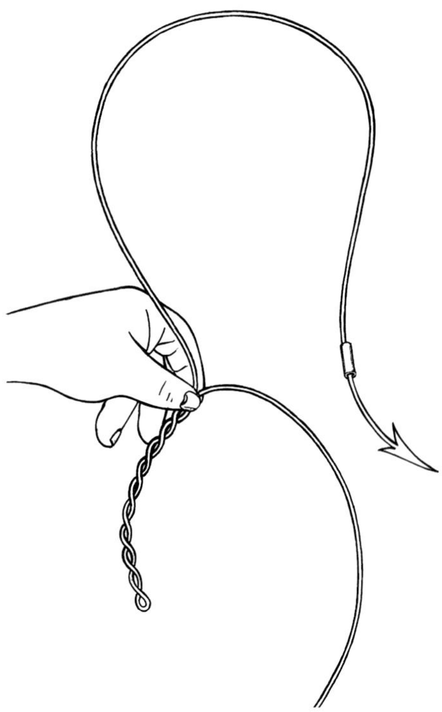

5. Here you can see me holding the twisted dropper so that it cannot come undone. What is not shown is that the loops are cut off so that the line, which is not part of the twisted dropper, can spin and straighten out. Please note that I have also put a sleeve onto the line above the dropper.

6. The sleeve is then threaded from each side, with opposite ends to isolate the twisted dropper loop effectively swapping top for bottom and vice versa.

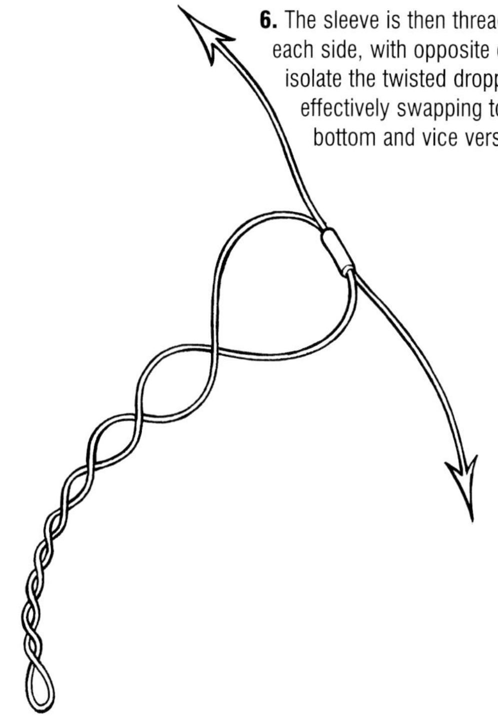

7. Crimp the sleeve securely with your crimping tool.

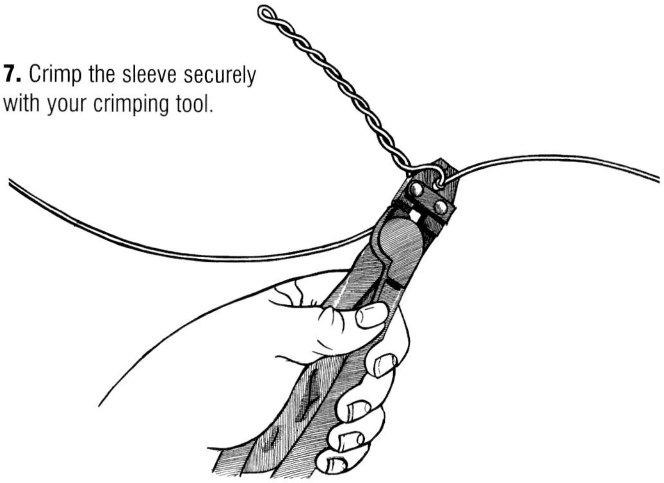

8. Attach your hook in the manner shown, taking care to thread the eye of the hook from the front.

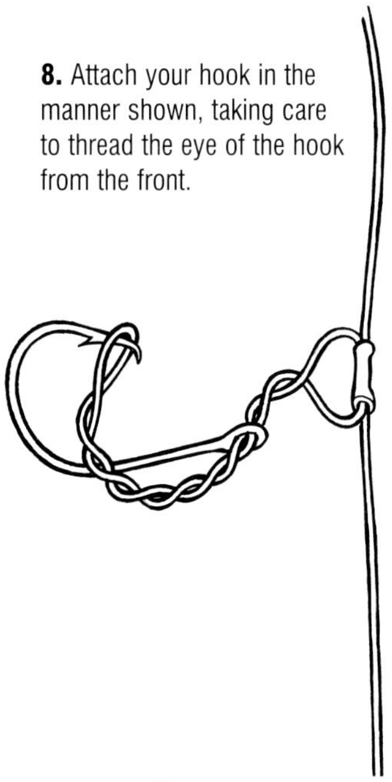

9. Add another sleeve and a suitably strong swivel to what is now the top of your rig.

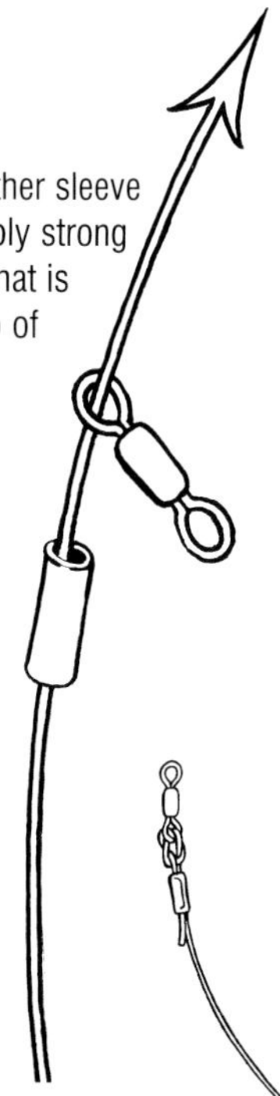

10. Tie an overhand knot in the wire or monofilament isolating the swivel. This is the first step in the formation of a Flemish Eye. Of course most folk will not bother and just fold the wire or mono over into a loop and crimp the sleeve over it, and that's OK: But I do like the security provided by the Flemish Eye.

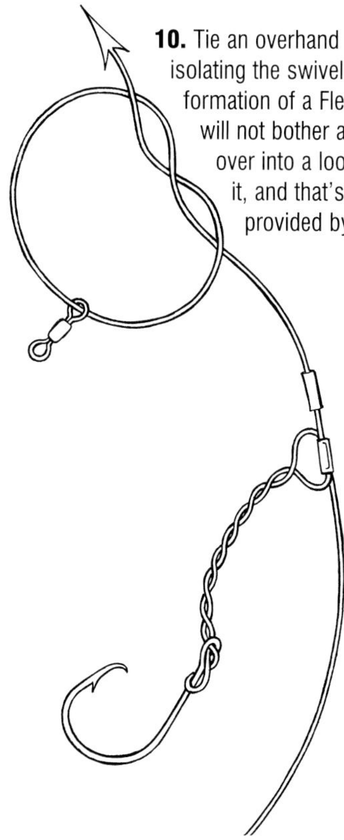

11. Thread the line or wire through the swivel once more and thread the tag through the sleeve.

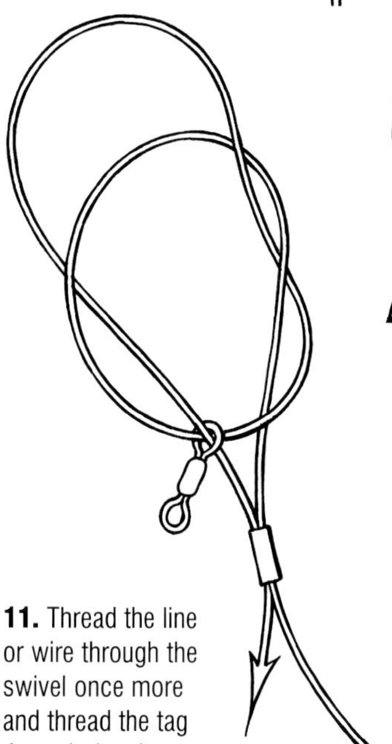

12. Close the Flemish Eye as tight as you can and crimp the sleeve securely up against it with your crimping tool.

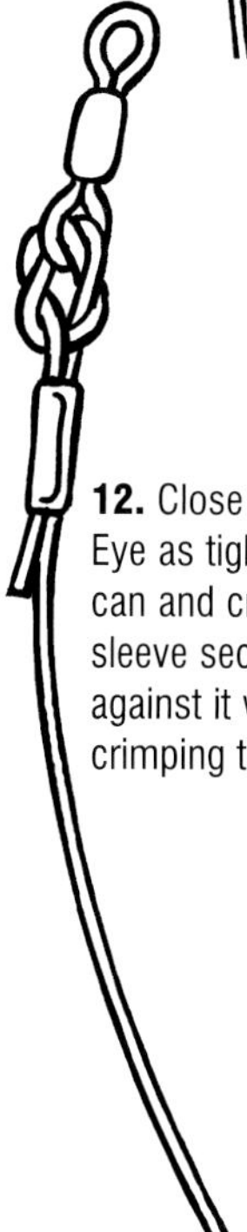

13. Repeat the process at the bottom, attaching a large wire clip to hold the sinker. Of course you could just make a large loop, and most do, but the clip is neat and strong and allows for the convenient joining of our modular rigs with single hooks, into multi-hook rigs.

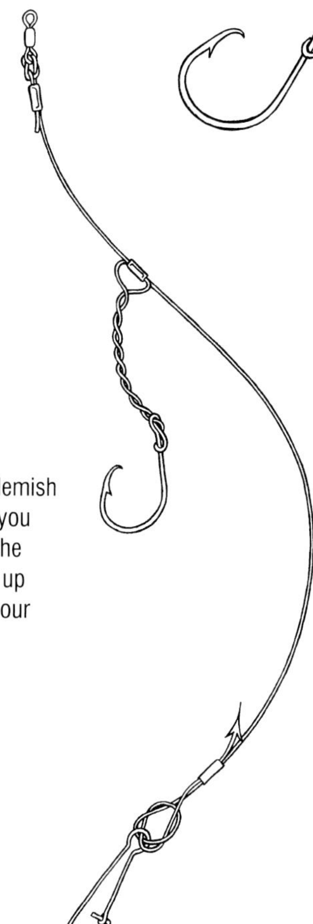

14. Another reason for this is because rigs with multiple hooks can become irretrievably tangled when more than one large fish is hooked at the one time. The problem is lessened somewhat when two or more rigs are joined together to present as many hooks (in respect to fishing regulations) as desired, with a swivel between each to lessen the tangling effect in that situation.

Chapter 4
FLOAT FISHING

Basic Float Fishing

This is a guide to identifying the intended purpose of various floats and how to rig them to fulfil that purpose.

The primary functions of fishing floats are to suspend a baited hook from the surface and to signal a bite. There are many types of commercially made floats which fit basically into two main categories, those designed to be fixed on the line and called fixed floats, and those that are designed to slide along the line with stoppers limiting their travel, either in one, or both directions.

Those designed to be fixed on the line include stem floats, quills, wagglers, pencil and spring loaded floats. Floats designed to run along the line have a hollow tube down the centre that allows them to slide.

Fixed Floats

Fixed floats are those designed to be fixed in position on the line so that the baited hook may be set at a predetermined depth each time it is cast out.

The two most satisfactory ways of fixing a float in position are first, the use of a plastic or rubber sleeve that is slipped over the top of the float's stem, and the line, once the bottom has been threaded. This method is most commonly used with quill floats and some bodied stem floats.

The other method is to first thread the bottom eye of the float with the line and crimp a small split-shot—or split shot and bead if the shot would have to be too large—onto the line each side of the eye to hold it in position. This method is used for waggler floats.

Spring loaded floats are also available. However, in my experience they do not hold their position on the line very well and tend to slip. Also, being used in water, the metal spring has a finite life. Use them if you wish, but I've found them disappointing.

Rigging with a Quill

Quill floats can be pulled beneath the surface with little resistance; that is why they are favoured for timid surface feeders that would be spooked on feeling the resistance of an aggressively buoyant float.

Early quill floats were made from porcupine quills or the flight feathers of large birds. A loop of bent wire, or some stiff fibre was bound at one end to form an eye, and a sleeve of some convenient material, including animal gut or the like, to slip over the line at the top of the float.

Nowadays quill floats are mass produced with an eye conveniently attached at the bottom and a rubber sleeve at the top that allows you to fix the float in place on the line. They are mostly used when fishing for comparatively small species like mullet, gar, balao, piper and needlefish.

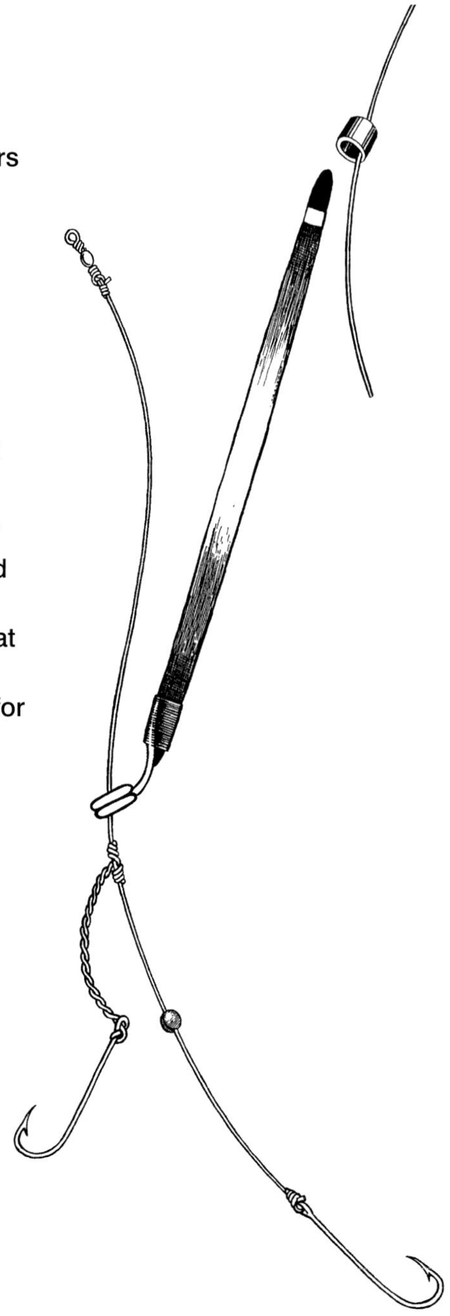

1. Shown is a representation of a commercially available quill float. I have drawn the eye larger than it really is so that other aspects of the rig can be more easily shown. The retaining sleeve is threaded with the line from your rod and reel. The rig is made up using knots we've previously described. The hook is usually a long shanked (for easy removal) size 8–12, the swivel is size 14, small enough to pass through the eye of the float. A small split shot is added to ballast the float so that it sits upright in the water.

2. The main line from your rod and reel is threaded through the rubber ring or tube then tied to the swivel on the rig.

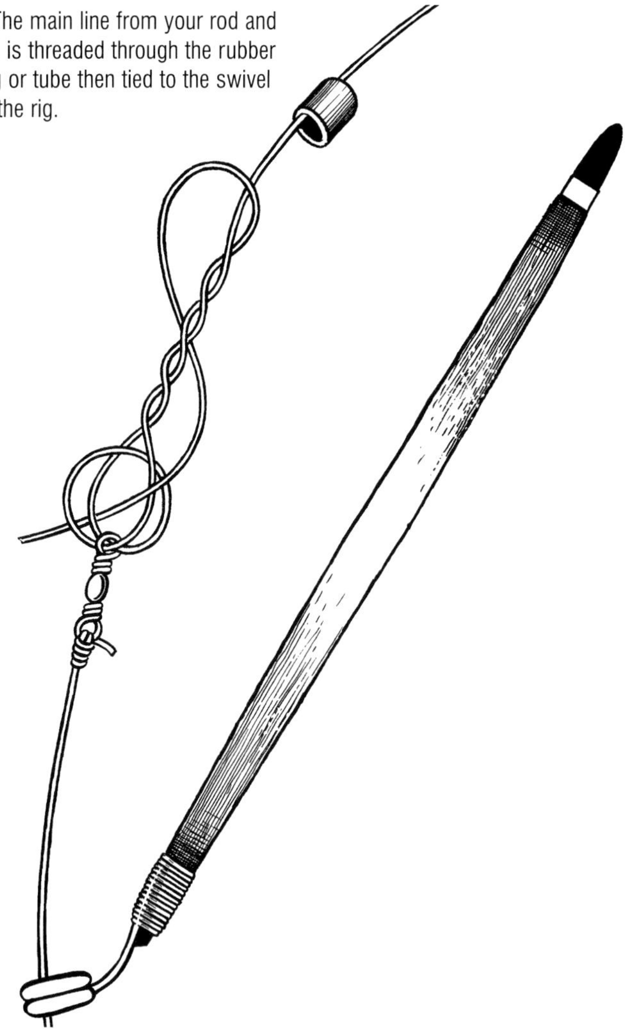

3. The depth at which the baited hooks are to be fished is determined and the retaining sleeve is pushed down over the top of the float and the line to fix it in position.

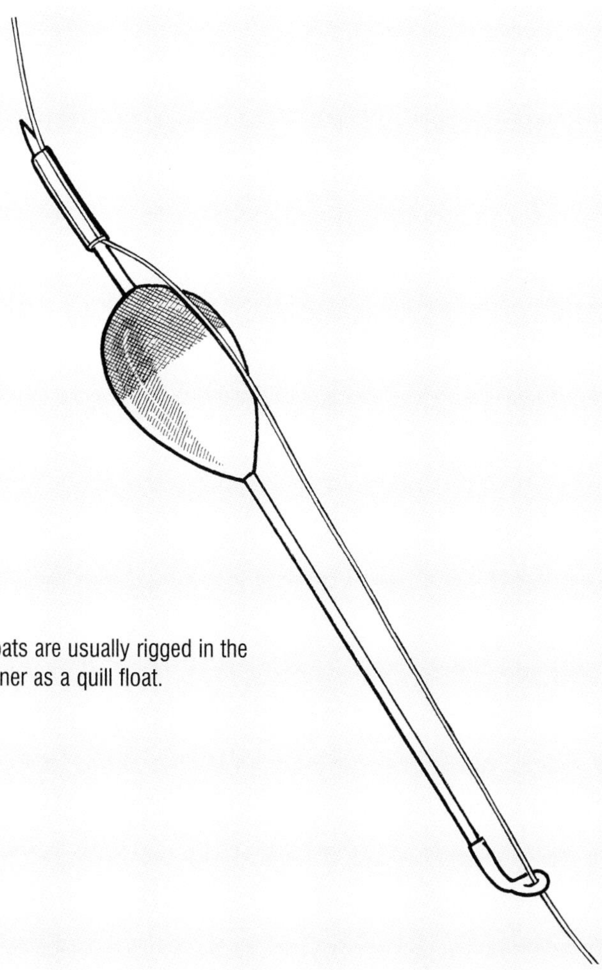

4. Stem floats are usually rigged in the same manner as a quill float.

Rigging with a Waggler Float

Attached to the line by the float's bottom eye only, waggler floats are so called because of the distinctive action they exhibit when compared with quills where the returning line is fixed at the top.

Once the depth at which the baited hook has been determined, and the corresponding length of line passed through the eye of the float, it is fixed in position by clamping two split shot onto the line, one either side of the float. More shot is used to ballast the float to your satisfaction.

Generally speaking, when ballasting with multiple split shot, the bulk of shot is placed on the line up toward the base of the float, diminishing down toward the hook. This arrangement is less likely to tangle when cast out.

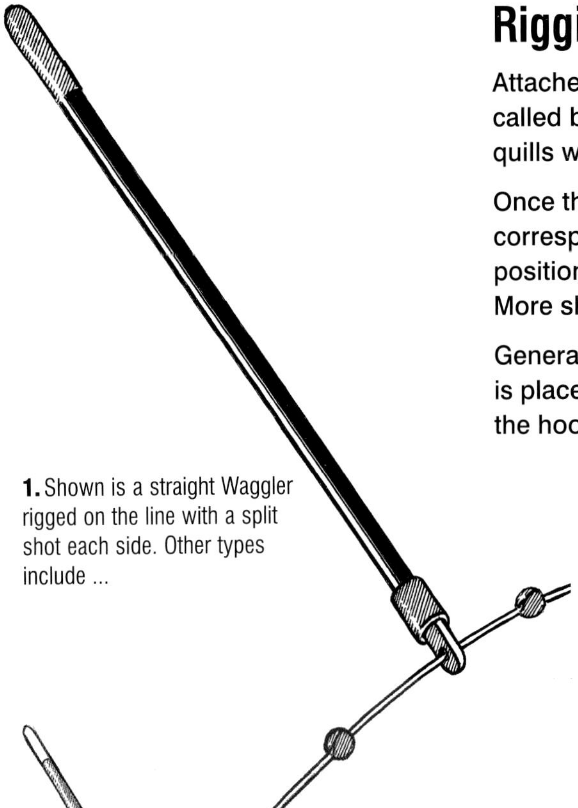

1. Shown is a straight Waggler rigged on the line with a split shot each side. Other types include ...

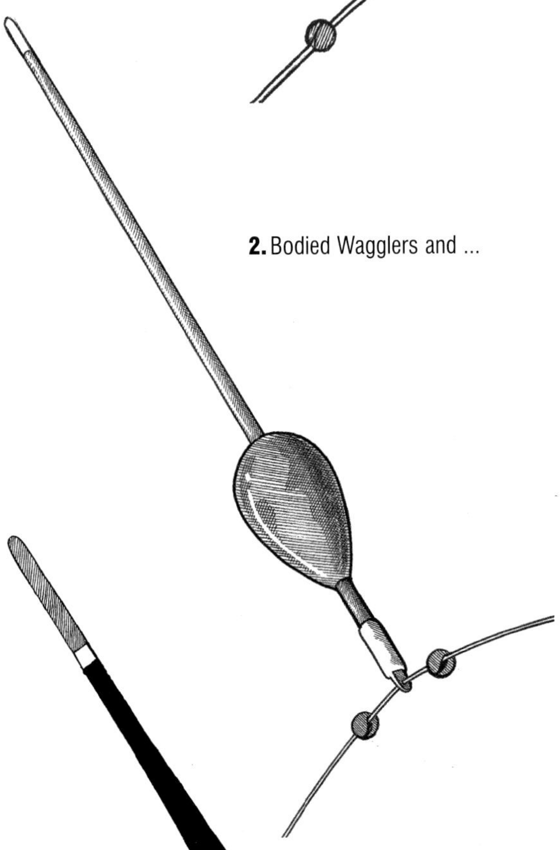

2. Bodied Wagglers and ...

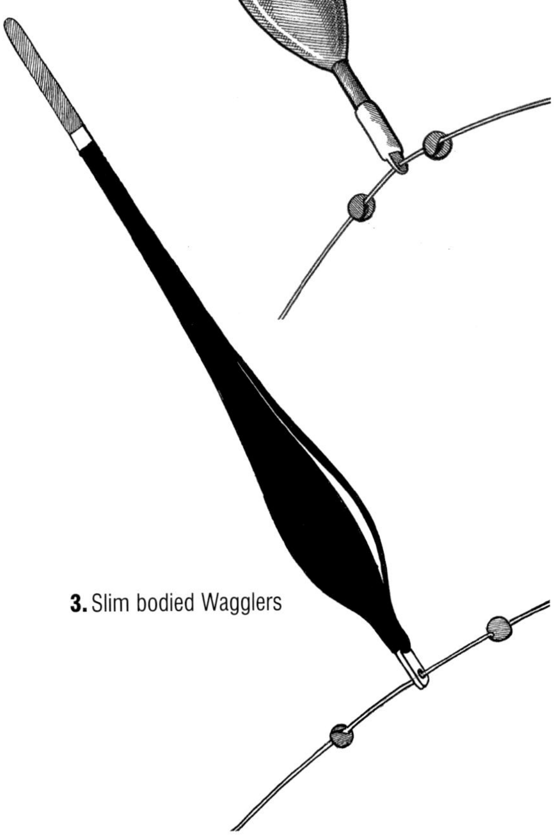

3. Slim bodied Wagglers

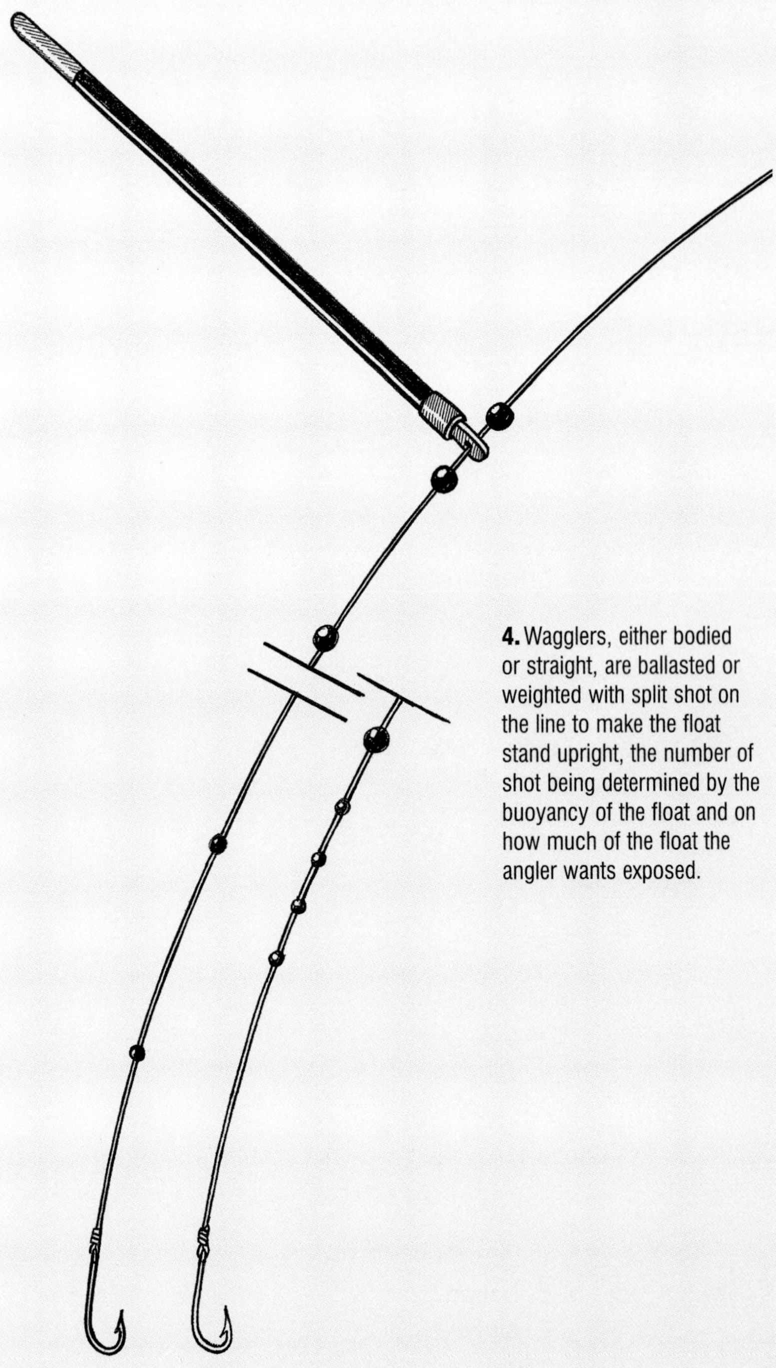

4. Wagglers, either bodied or straight, are ballasted or weighted with split shot on the line to make the float stand upright, the number of shot being determined by the buoyancy of the float and on how much of the float the angler wants exposed.

Spring Loaded Floats

Despite their shortcomings, fixed floats that hold their position on the line by means of a spring loaded device, are extremely popular with anglers fishing from piers. The most popular of all are the spherical plastic bob floats that come in a variety of sizes and are usually red and white in colour.

Their method of use is simplicity itself. The spring is depressed. Extending a hook that traps the line when the spring is released, determining the depth at which the bait is to be presented. The only trouble is that they tend to slip along the line. This may be avoided by clamping the float onto a loop that has been tied in the line.

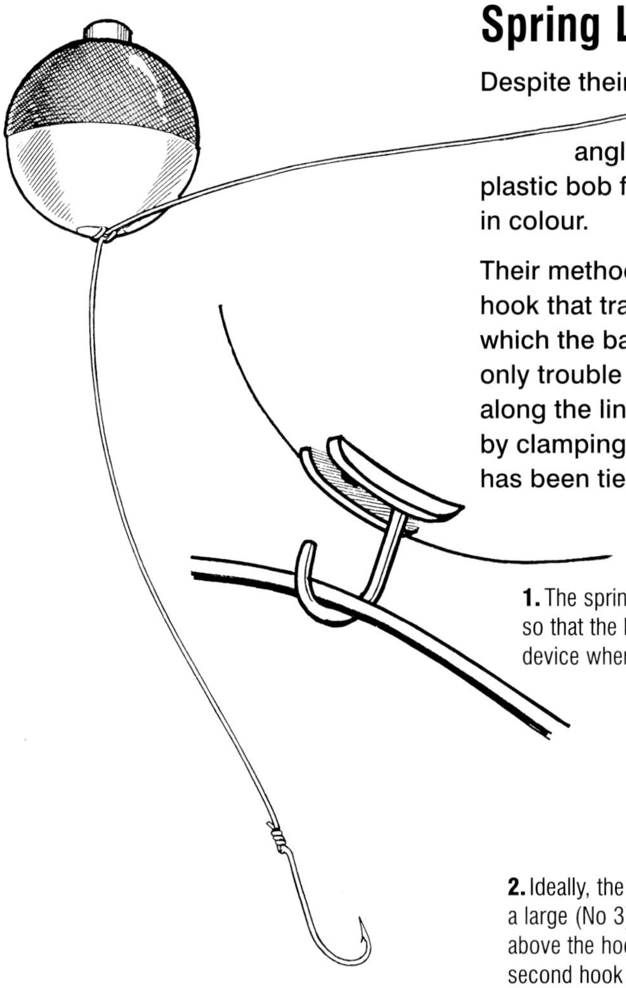

1. The spring on the float is depressed so that the line is trapped by the device when the spring is released.

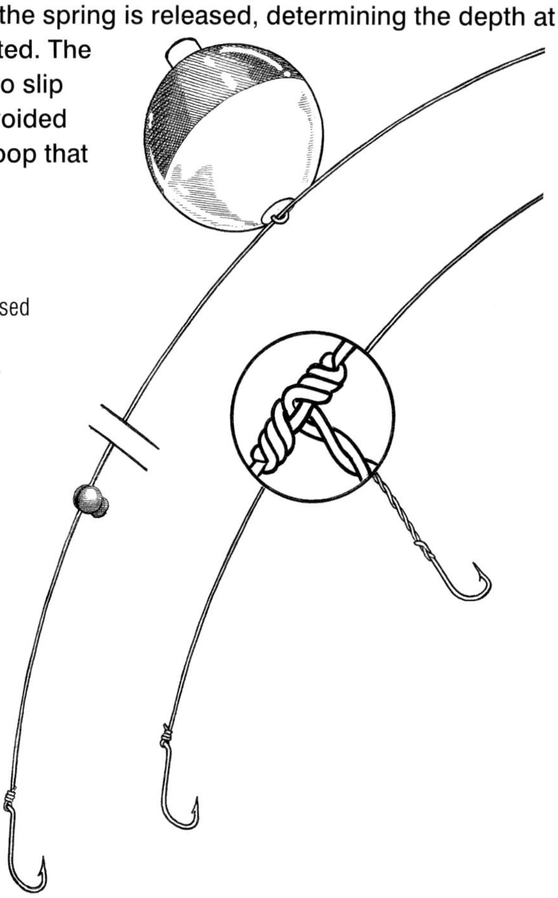

2. Ideally, the rig is weighted with a large (No 3) removable split shot above the hook. This rig features a second hook that has been attached with a Twisted Dropper Loop to prevent one tangling around the other.

Running Floats

Running floats are used when the depth at which the bait is to be presented is greater than the maximum drop, from the rod tip, that could be cast effectively.

One example would be an angler who wanted to present a bait, alive or dead, some 30 feet (9 metres) beneath the surface of the water from a rock ledge or pier in deep water.

You wouldn't be able to cast with such a long leader, however—with a running float rigged to slide freely along the line between a stopper knot, small enough to be wound through the guides, or baited hook on which rests a small sinker—the rig may be cast out easily. Let's look at making a rig to do that.

Materials:

- *Apart from the line you intend to rig, you will need a fair size float, one with a hollow tube down the centre from top to bottom to permit it to slide along the line.*
- *Running floats, although they come in a variety of sizes and shapes, some weighed, some not, the defining characteristic is the tube through the centre through which the line is threaded.*
- *You will also need a bead like those 0.2 inch (5 mm) coloured plastic beads you can buy from fishing tackle stores. The bead is to prevent the stopper knot from sliding right through the float after it hits the water.*
- *Finally, you will need about 15 inches (40 cm) of another line, preferably about half the strength of your main line. This is to make the Nail Knot we are going to tie use as a stopper that can be wound in through the guides on your rod, and—when it's tied with a line that is somewhat lighter than the main line—it will be permanent and will not slip up or down the line.*

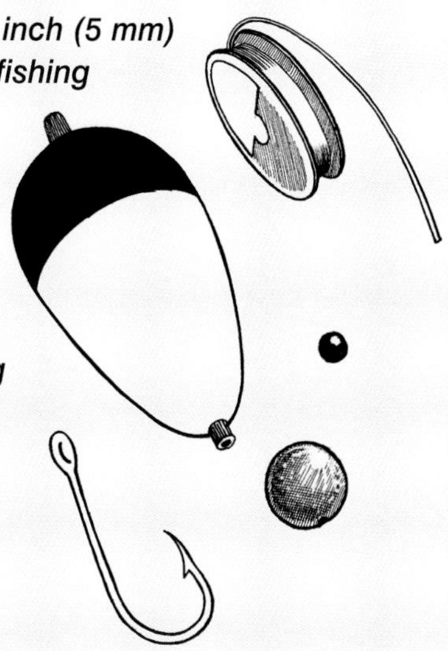

Running Floats cont.

While there are various running float rigs, this one demonstrates the principle on which most others are based.

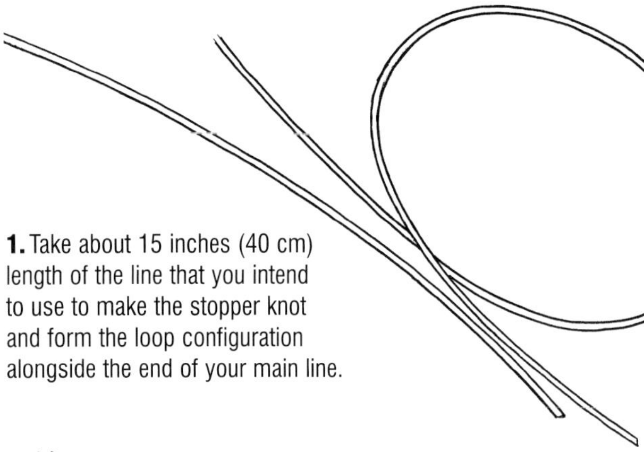

1. Take about 15 inches (40 cm) length of the line that you intend to use to make the stopper knot and form the loop configuration alongside the end of your main line.

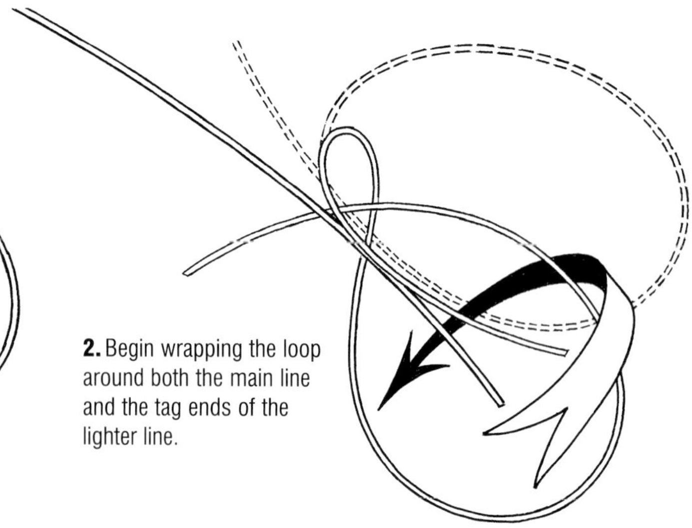

2. Begin wrapping the loop around both the main line and the tag ends of the lighter line.

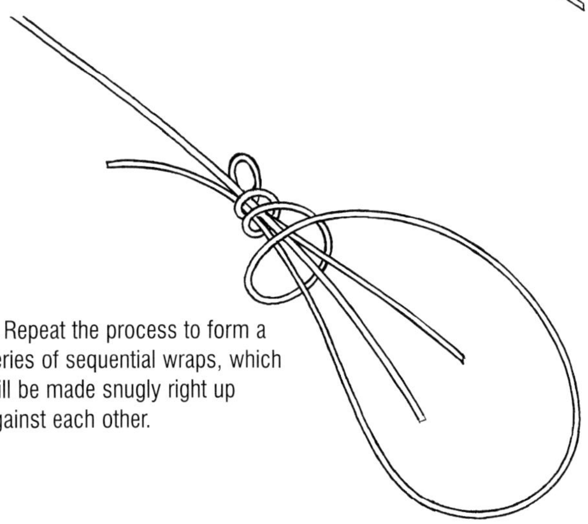

3. Repeat the process to form a series of sequential wraps, which will be made snugly right up against each other.

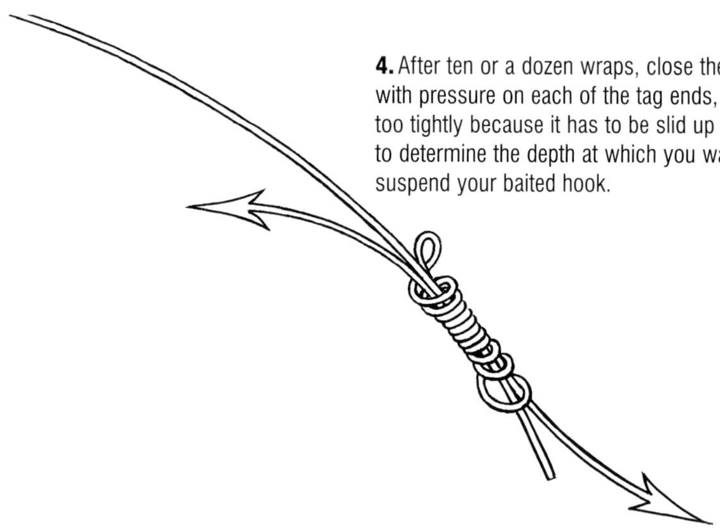

4. After ten or a dozen wraps, close the knot with pressure on each of the tag ends, but not too tightly because it has to be slid up the line to determine the depth at which you want to suspend your baited hook.

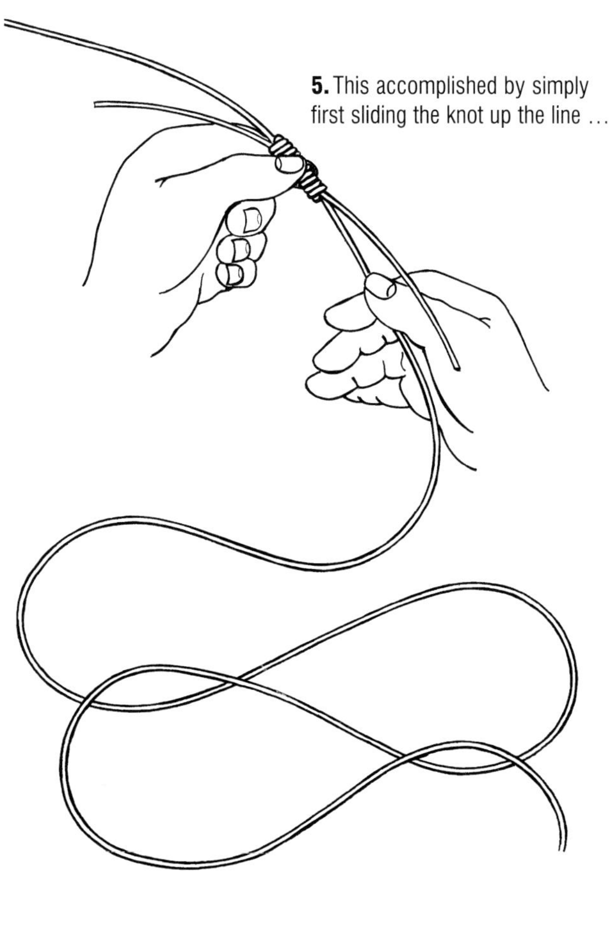

5. This accomplished by simply first sliding the knot up the line …

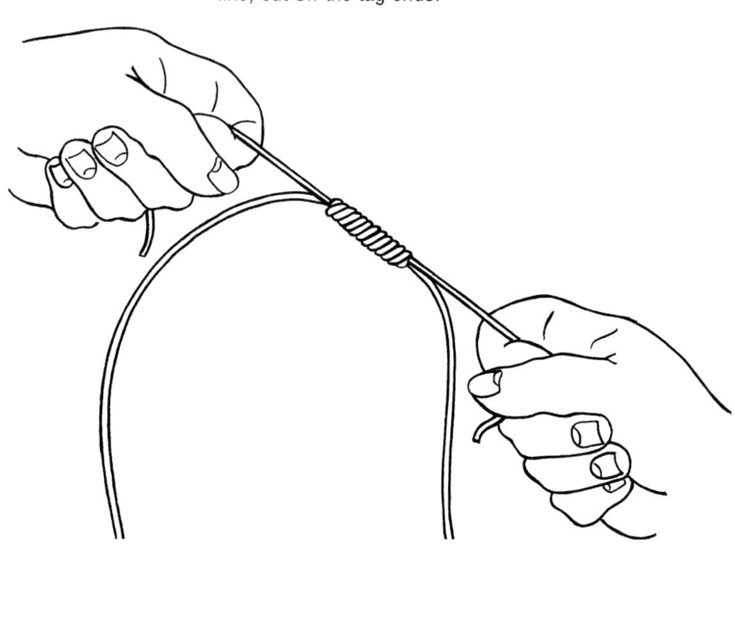

6. And then pulling the knot tight at a predetermined point that you could mark with a felt pen or something. After the knot has locked down on the line, cut off the tag ends.

7. The next step is to thread the bead, float and ball sinker onto your line in that order.

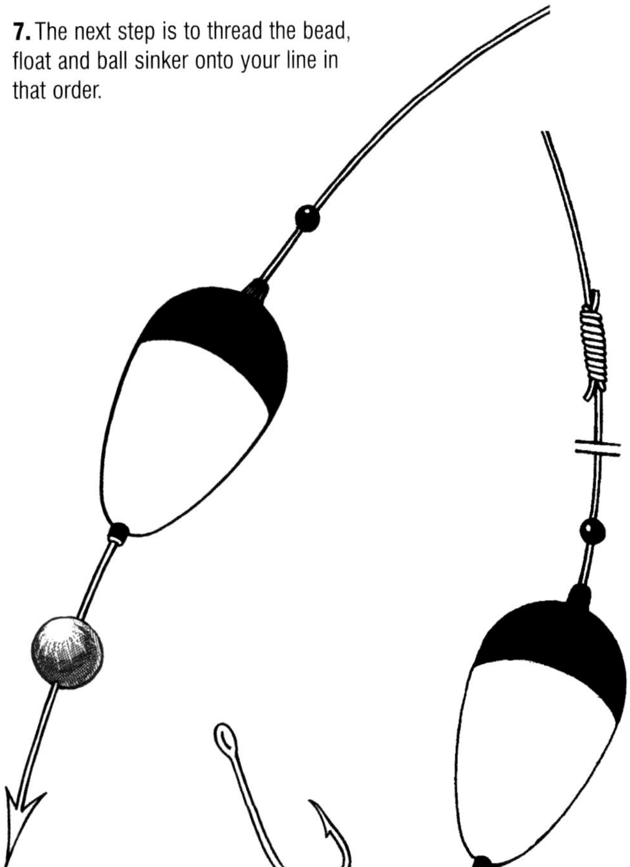

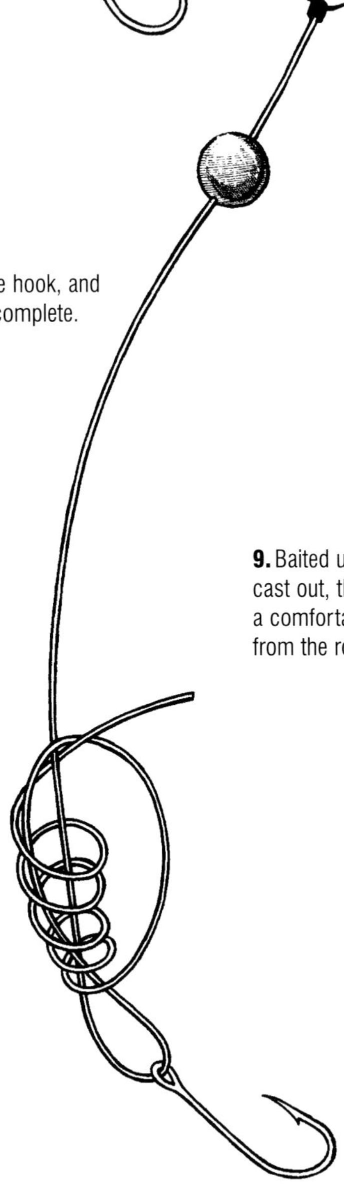

8. Tie on the hook, and your rig is complete.

9. Baited up and ready to cast out, the rig hangs a comfortable distance from the rod tip.

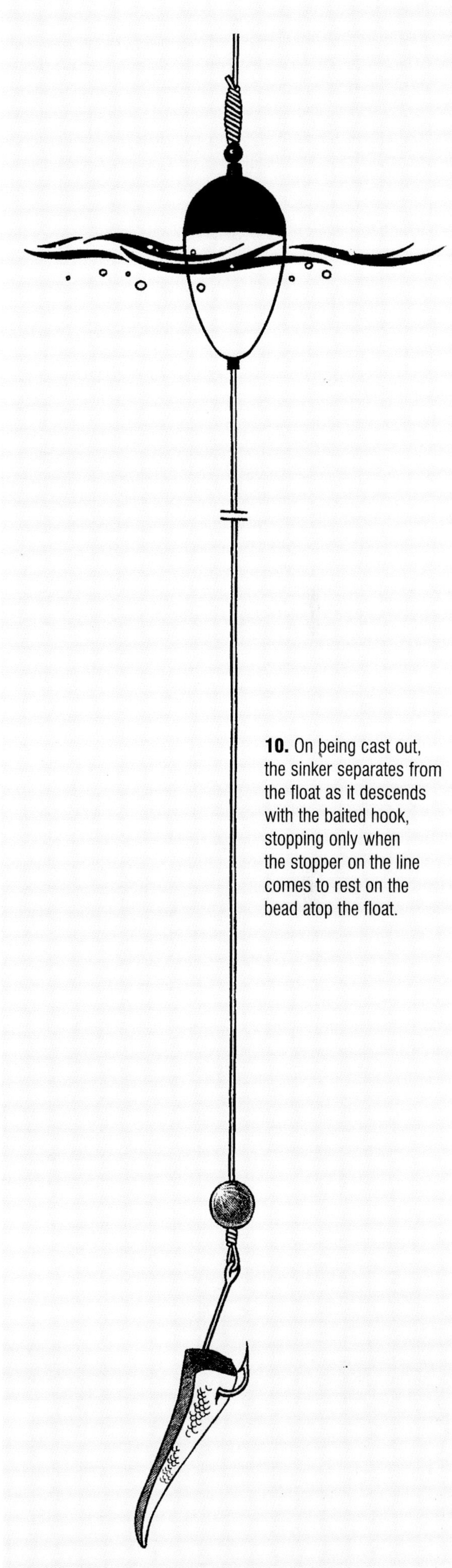

10. On being cast out, the sinker separates from the float as it descends with the baited hook, stopping only when the stopper on the line comes to rest on the bead atop the float.

Tandem Floats

Bubble Floats

Bubble floats are designed as running floats to be rigged in tandem with a second smaller float—usually a small styrene foam ball float through which the line is threaded and—from which the bait is suspended. Bubble floats are mainly used in slow flowing or still water for trout.

It is a mistake to fix a bubble float to the line, even though some are packaged with the means to do so. For a bubble float to fulfil its correct function it must be free to slide along the line. If your bubble float submerges or moves significantly when a fish takes the bait then the bubble float is incorrectly rigged and not fulfilling the purpose for which it was designed.

Although there are a variety of creatively designed bubble floats on the market—some coloured, others with rings for attachment to the line; some even with line jamming devices and eyelets—those of use to serious anglers are fairly large, perhaps of similar shape and size to that of a bantam's egg, and made of clear plastic to minimize silhouette and shadow.

There is, or should be, a central tube running through the float from end to end (top to bottom). This tube, through which the line must run freely, is displaced to enable water to be drizzled into the float. This is to provide sufficient weight for the cast. The secondary float, the styrene foam ball float in this case, provides the bottom stopper. There is no top stopper on this rig.

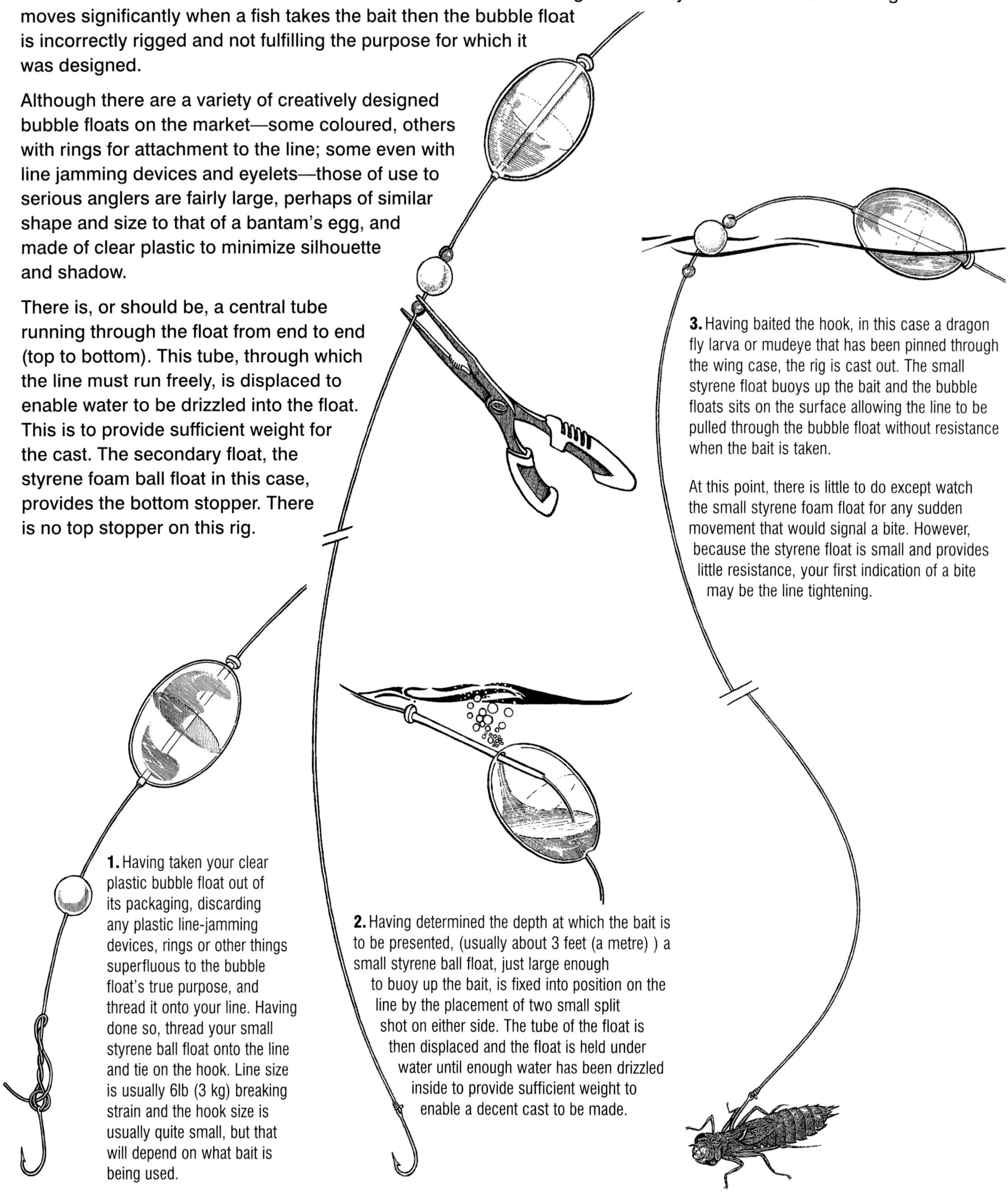

3. Having baited the hook, in this case a dragon fly larva or mudeye that has been pinned through the wing case, the rig is cast out. The small styrene float buoys up the bait and the bubble floats sits on the surface allowing the line to be pulled through the bubble float without resistance when the bait is taken.

At this point, there is little to do except watch the small styrene foam float for any sudden movement that would signal a bite. However, because the styrene float is small and provides little resistance, your first indication of a bite may be the line tightening.

1. Having taken your clear plastic bubble float out of its packaging, discarding any plastic line-jamming devices, rings or other things superfluous to the bubble float's true purpose, and thread it onto your line. Having done so, thread your small styrene ball float onto the line and tie on the hook. Line size is usually 6lb (3 kg) breaking strain and the hook size is usually quite small, but that will depend on what bait is being used.

2. Having determined the depth at which the bait is to be presented, (usually about 3 feet (a metre)) a small styrene ball float, just large enough to buoy up the bait, is fixed into position on the line by the placement of two small split shot on either side. The tube of the float is then displaced and the float is held under water until enough water has been drizzled inside to provide sufficient weight to enable a decent cast to be made.

Berley Cage Floats

Berley cage floats are used in the sea to catch garfish, piper, balao, needlefish and other surface feeders.

Like the bubble float, berley cage floats are rigged in tandem with a second float (In this case a bodied waggler) that is fixed in position on the line at a predetermined distance (3 feet (a metre)) above the hook or hooks.

The rig is produced by first threading the line through the berley cage float then through the eye of the second float; the hook is then tied onto the end of the line.

The depth at which the baited hook is to be suspended is determined and fixed by clamping a split shot onto the line on either side of the waggler. Split shot is then placed on the line below the float to provide sufficient ballast to right the float.

With no swivel or other stopping device on the line above the berley cage float, fish can pull line through the berley cage float and not be spooked by its considerable resistance.

1. Shown is a Berley cage float rigged in tandem with a secondary float that is securely fixed to the line and which acts as a bite indicator. There are two hooks on the rig, the second hook being attached with a twisted dropper loop to minimise tangling. Additional weight is added to the rig with split shot.

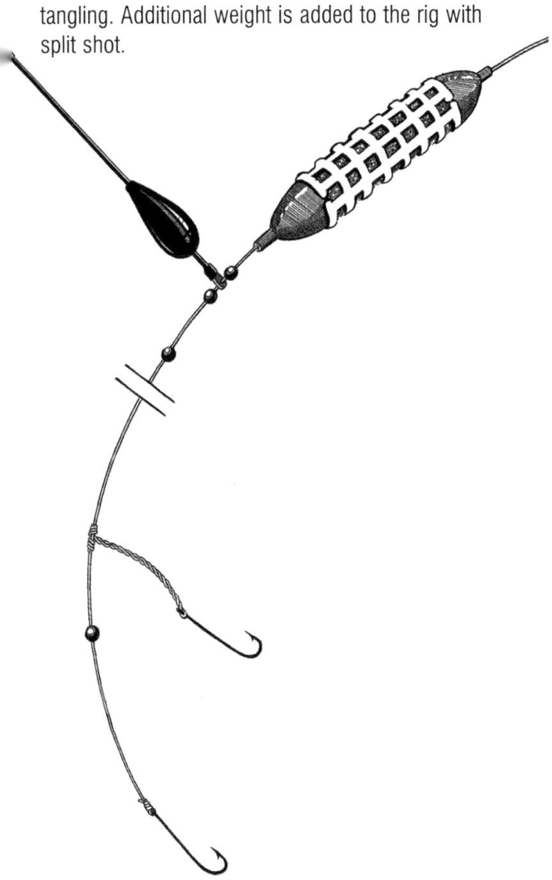

Controllers

Controllers or surface-controllers are forward-weighted, cigar-shaped floats designed for making long casts. Commercially produced from hollow plastic with a lead weight at the bottom and an eye at the top to attach the line they are generally available in sizes from 1/8 to 5/8 oz (3 to 20 grams) with applications in both fresh and salt water. They are favoured by freshwater carp fishing enthusiasts who may own many in different sizes and configurations. We will look at just one that is representative.

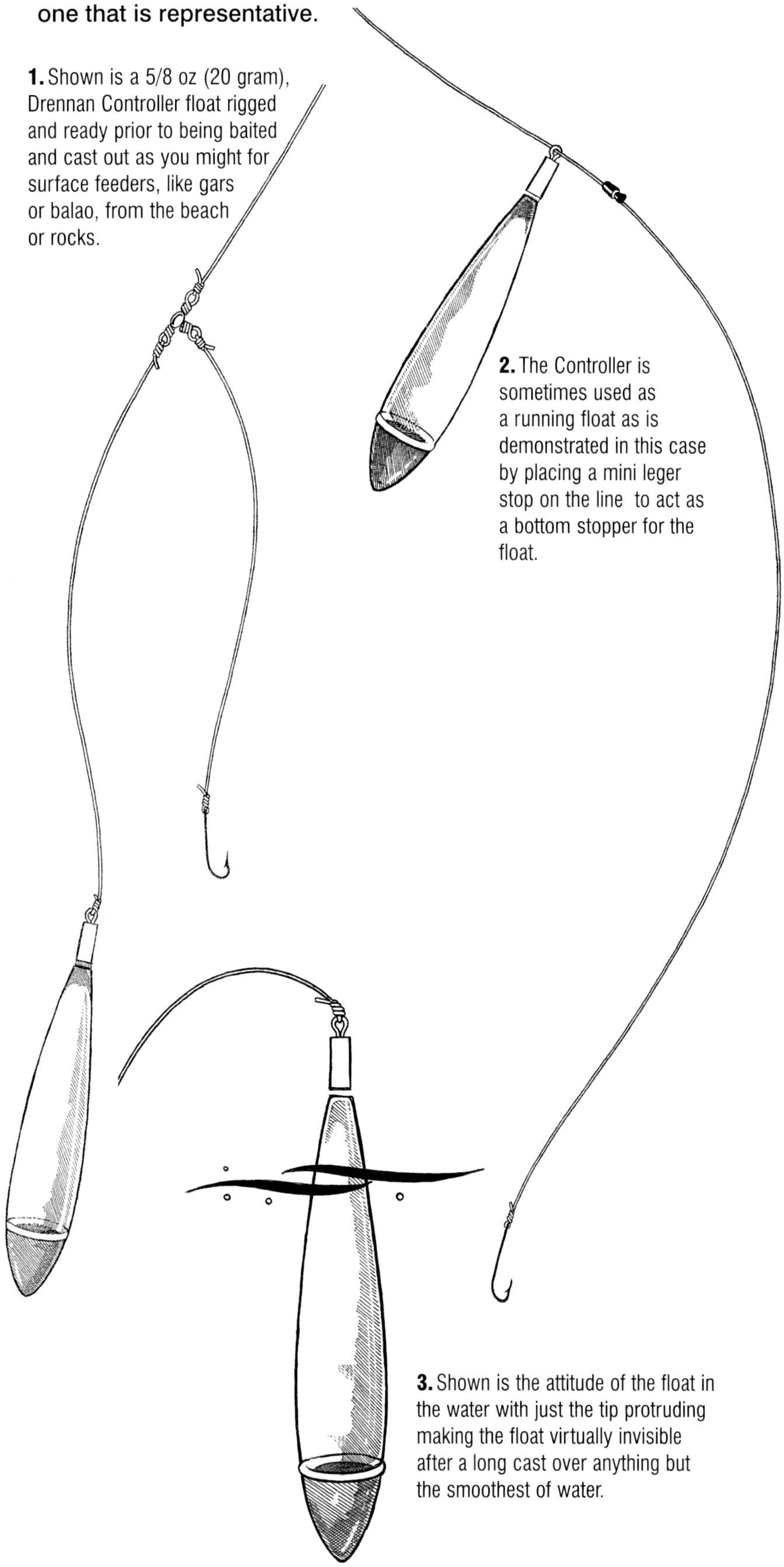

1. Shown is a 5/8 oz (20 gram), Drennan Controller float rigged and ready prior to being baited and cast out as you might for surface feeders, like gars or balao, from the beach or rocks.

2. The Controller is sometimes used as a running float as is demonstrated in this case by placing a mini leger stop on the line to act as a bottom stopper for the float.

3. Shown is the attitude of the float in the water with just the tip protruding making the float virtually invisible after a long cast over anything but the smoothest of water.

Chapter 5
MULTIPLE HOOKS

Rigging with Multiple Hooks

Baited hooks catch fish and they are most effective when the size of bait is compatible with the size of the hook, which in turn is compatible with the size of the line being used: Common sense really.

However, it is sometimes productive to use quite large baits on relatively light tackle. Using a larger hook is not the answer because the larger the hook, the more difficult it is to set with light tackle. The answer is to use more than one normal size hook in the same bait.

The practice of linking hooks together by opening the eye, passing the point and spear of the next hook, through that open eye. Then closing the eye, provides a basic but effective linkage of those hooks.

The opening of the eye is tricky and led to the development of cone piers, but the quality of cone pliers varies a good deal and the first set I bought, the cones designed to open the eyes of the hooks for ganging were of soft metal and soon became worn and useless.

The next two sets of cone pliers I bought met an even more ignominious fate when one of handles snapped off each under the pressure of opening the eyes of hooks. I'm not that strong; neither were the piers.

Fortunately, several hook manufacturers make hooks with the eyes already opened for this very purpose and they are readily available through most fishing tackle outlets.

Those that I have used and found to be effective include the Mustad 4202D (which has a turned down eye) and the Mustad 4200D (which has a straight eye). There's a variety others to choose from.

Making a Flight of Ganged Hooks

1. Ganging hooks together is simple when using hooks supplied with open eyes.

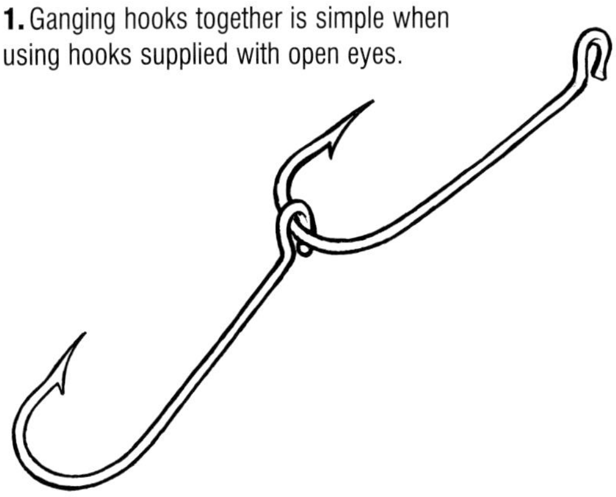

2. You can link two, three or more hooks together this way, securing each in turn by closing the eyes with a pair of pliers.

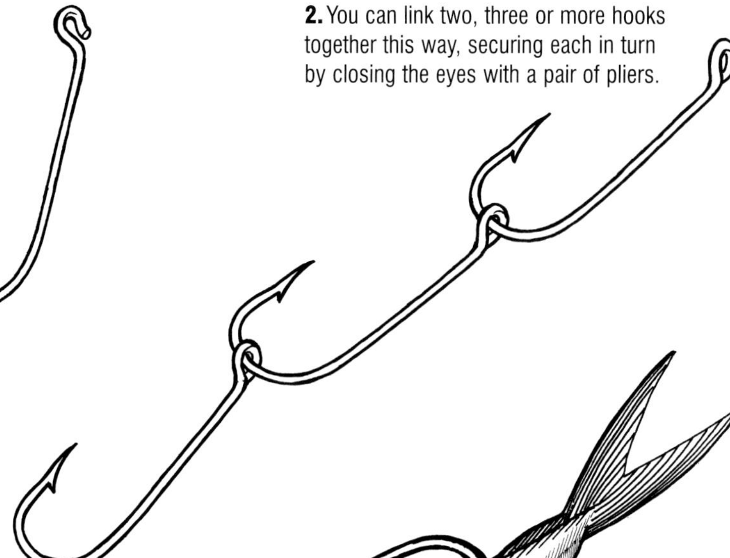

3. Having assembled a flight of ganged hooks, four in this case, you can present a whole baitfish or strip of squid in a manner both attractive and deadly.

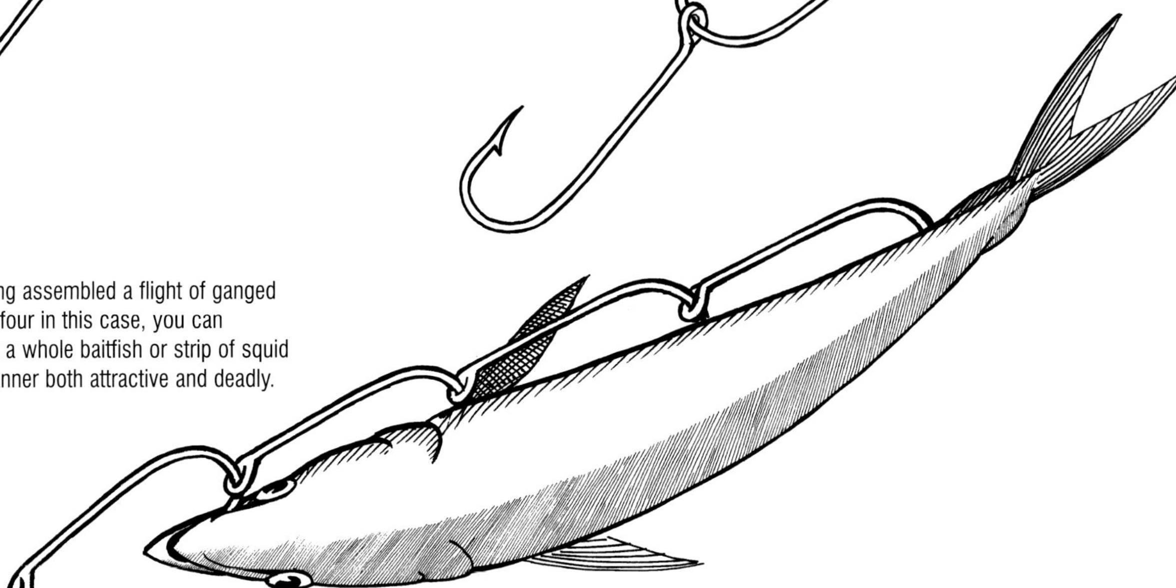

Making Flexible Flights of Hooks with Swivels in between

Ganged hooks are rather stiff and require some skill to bait. However, linking the hooks with swivels makes the flight of ganged hooks flexible and easy to use.

The idea of using swivels to link hooks together is not new. Hooks may be linked by threading small swivels over the wire of an open eye hook and – once the eye of the hook has been closed – retained between the eye and the barb and barb of the hook.

Flights of ganged hooks made in the way are elegant and flexible and very satisfying to use. However, their strength is limited by the size of the swivel, which is no problem if the swivels used are of the very finest quality. Mostly the swivels used for this purpose are not and herein lies a potential weakness.

The use of vinyl plastic, or very tough rubber tubing. permits the use of much larger swivels as the link. This not only makes the flight of ganged hooks utterly flexible, the use of larger, stronger swivels extends the length of the flight of hooks so that fewer hooks may be used.

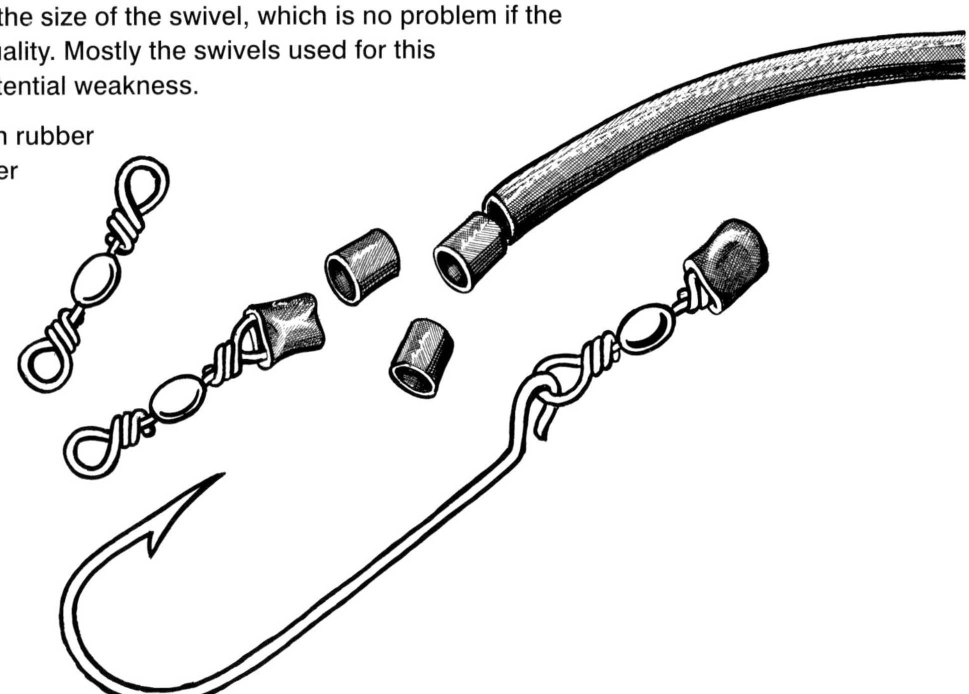

1. Here is a representation of the following items: Size 6/0 open eye hooks and a length of 1/6 inch (4 mm) vinyl tubing from which some short sections have been cut. These are fitted over the eye of swivels marked size 4 and the swivel is looped over the wire of the open eye. You may care to use different combinations.

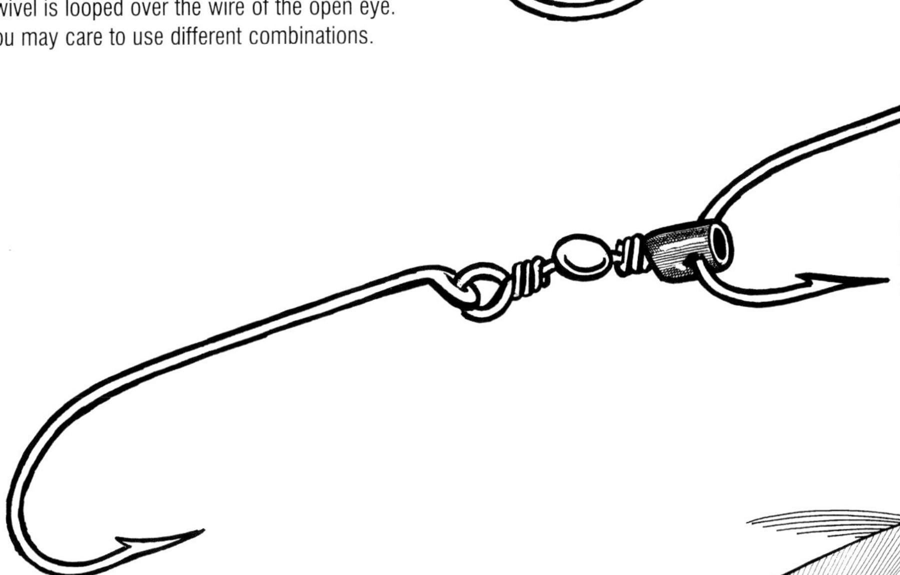

2. Shown here is the linking of two hooks by first closing the eye of one over the swivel then pushing the point and spear of the next hook through the vinyl sleeve and the eye of the swivel. Continuing thus you can make a flexible flight of several hooks.

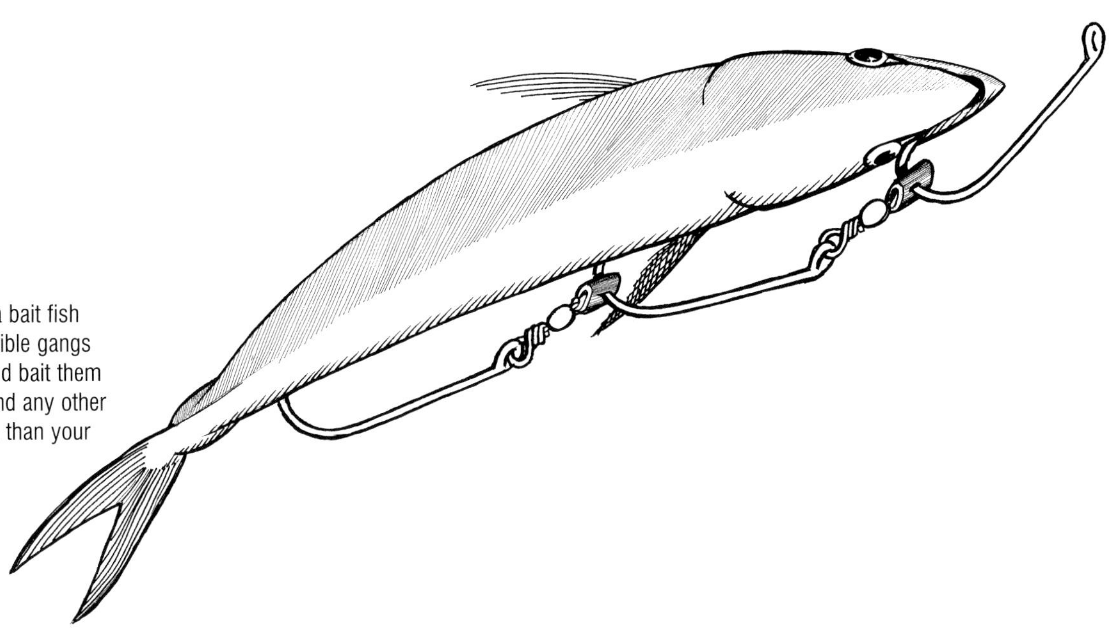

3. Shown is a representation of a bait fish on such a rig. You can make flexible gangs (flexi-gangs) of different sizes and bait them with small fish, strips of squid and any other suitable bait and catch more fish than your companions.

Simple Snelling

The Simple Snell is used for making fixed, multiple hook rigs. You need hooks with either down-turned (eye bent toward the point) or upturned eyes (eye bent away from the point) for the most satisfactory result.

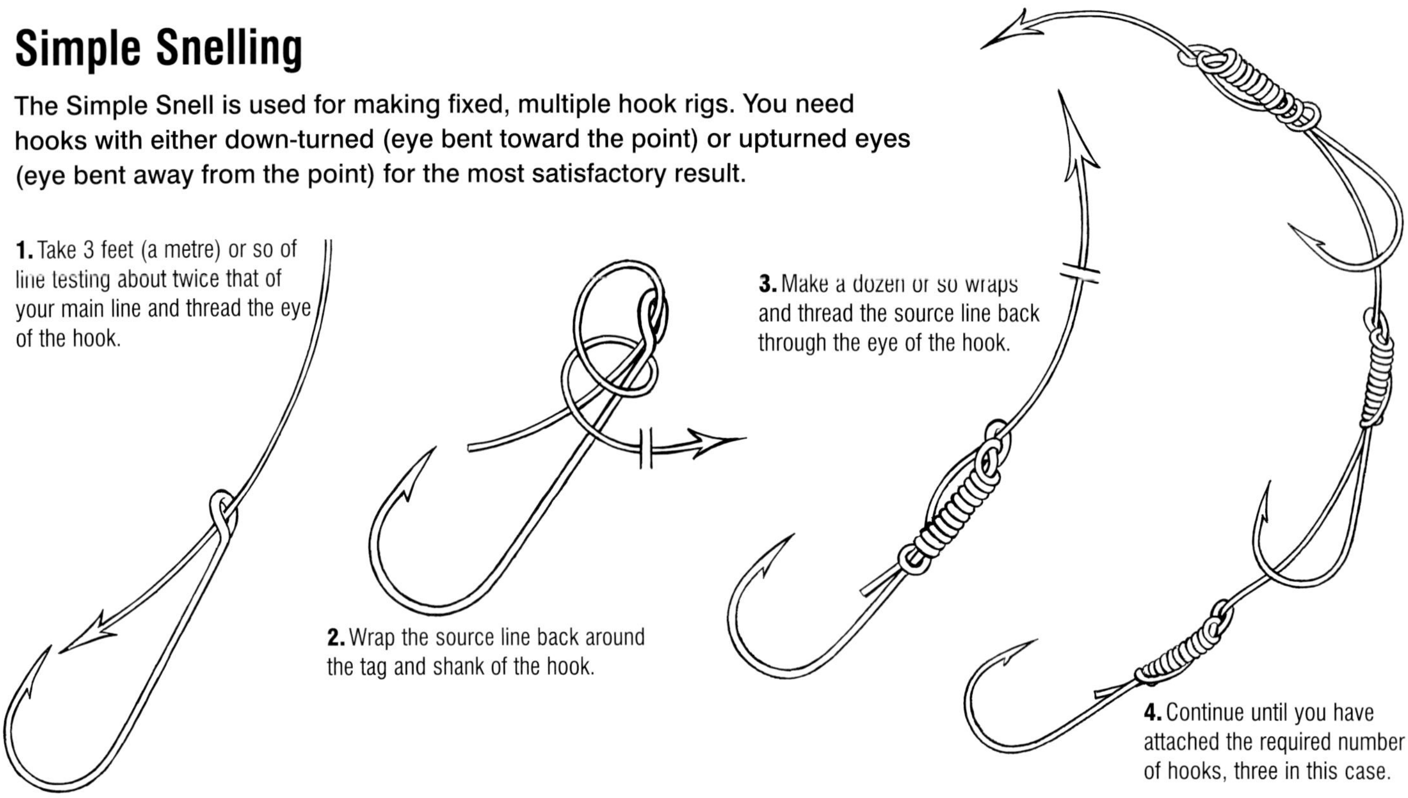

1. Take 3 feet (a metre) or so of line testing about twice that of your main line and thread the eye of the hook.

2. Wrap the source line back around the tag and shank of the hook.

3. Make a dozen or so wraps and thread the source line back through the eye of the hook.

4. Continue until you have attached the required number of hooks, three in this case.

Adjustable Two Hook Rig

Probably the most effective rig I have ever used when bottom fishing over sand or mud for big snapper and mulloway, at anchor in relatively shallow water up to 60 feet (20 metres), is this adjustable two hook rig and leader. It is designed to be used with a running sinker rig described on page 9 or the Pulley Rig on page 35.

You will need some stiff vinyl or plastic tubing that will fit through the eye of the adjustable hook like the size 4/0 beak or octopus pattern hooks that I use. I have used lumo tube from fishing tackle stores and 1/12 inch (2 mm) vinyl tube that you can get from haberdasheries.

You will need two hooks, one preferably larger than the other. I suggest a 4/0 beak hook as the slider and a 6/0 circle as the fixed hook at the end, but you can use sizes 6/0 and 8/0 should you be fishing with larger baits or hoping for a very large fish.

I use 60 pound nylon monofilament as leader material for the leader, but you could use fluorocarbon if you felt there was an advantage in doing so.

You will also need some lighter line for the binding on the tubing. You could use the same material as the leader if you wanted, but I found the use of a finer line say 0.02 inch (0.5 mm) to be neater and easier to work with.

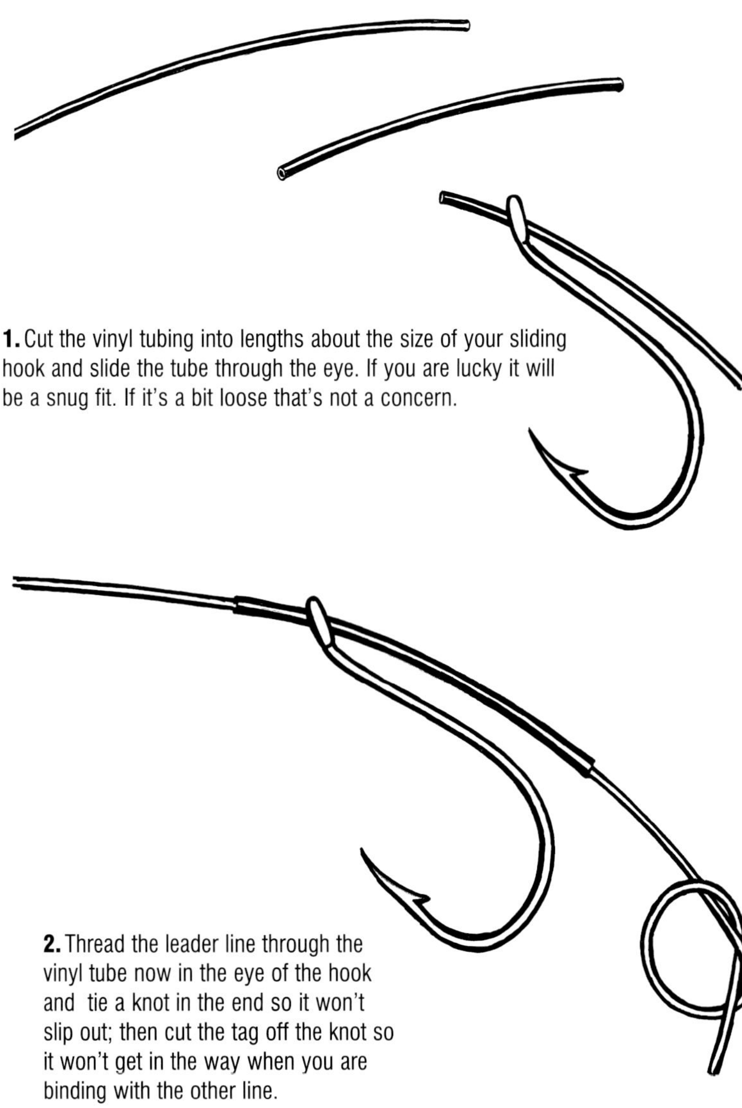

1. Cut the vinyl tubing into lengths about the size of your sliding hook and slide the tube through the eye. If you are lucky it will be a snug fit. If it's a bit loose that's not a concern.

2. Thread the leader line through the vinyl tube now in the eye of the hook and tie a knot in the end so it won't slip out; then cut the tag off the knot so it won't get in the way when you are binding with the other line.

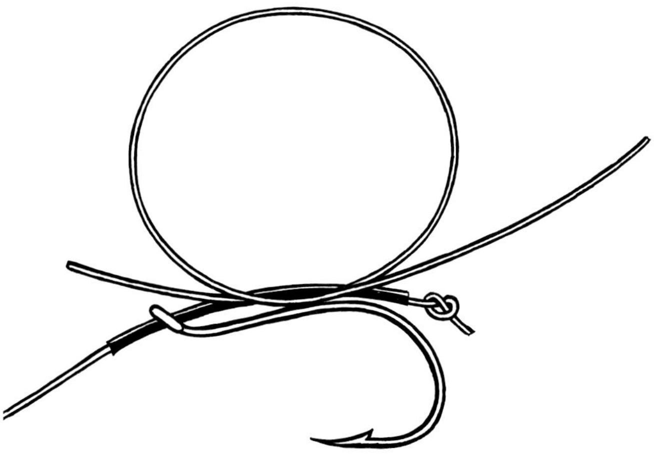

3. Taking a generous length of the lighter line (15 inches (40 cm) for a start until you become familiar with the operation) and make a loop alongside the hook, the same as we did when making the stopper knot for the running float back on page 22.

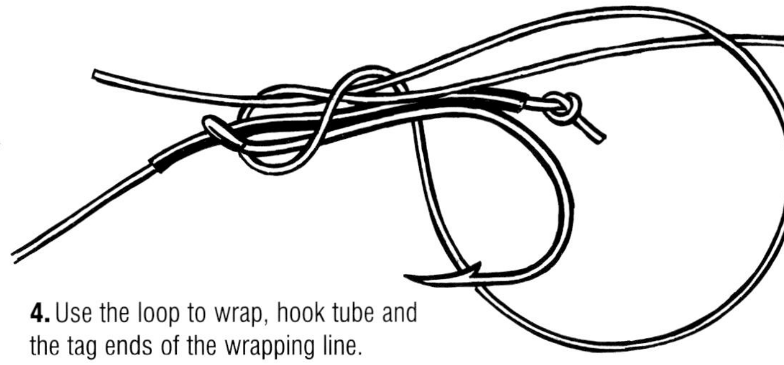

4. Use the loop to wrap, hook tube and the tag ends of the wrapping line.

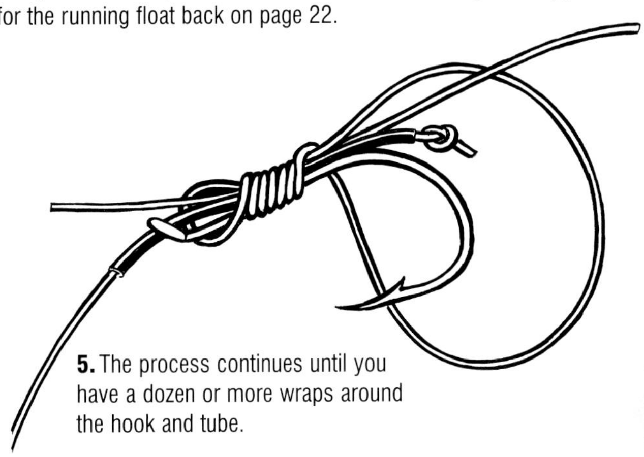

5. The process continues until you have a dozen or more wraps around the hook and tube.

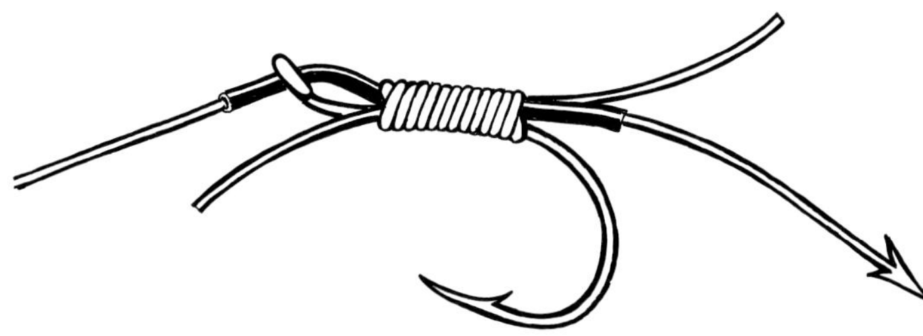

6. Pull gently on each tag end in turn to close up the loops at each end of the wrapping, then pull the binding tight. Check that the hook will slide along the line but under pressure, if it's too loose you will need to tighten it some more. When the hook slides under pressure, trim of the tags from the binding.

Of course we could simply tie the second hook, the one that is fixed to the end of the line, using one of the knots we have already discussed. However, at this stage I am going to introduce another knot that is particularly useful when tying hooks and other metal fitting to heavier lines; so cut off the safety knot and pull 3 feet (90 cm) of leader through the sliding hook and you are ready for the next step.

Nail Knot with a Loop

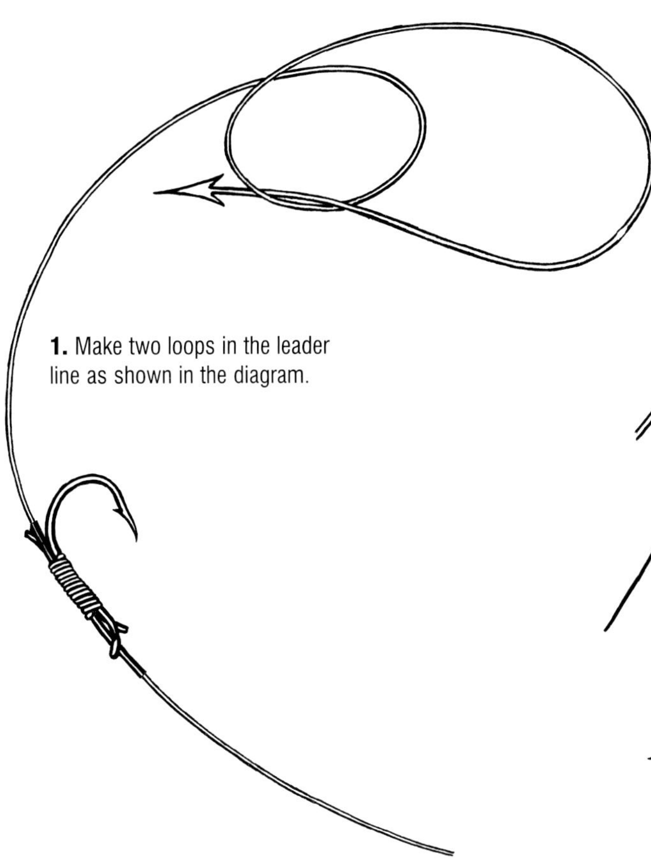

1. Make two loops in the leader line as shown in the diagram.

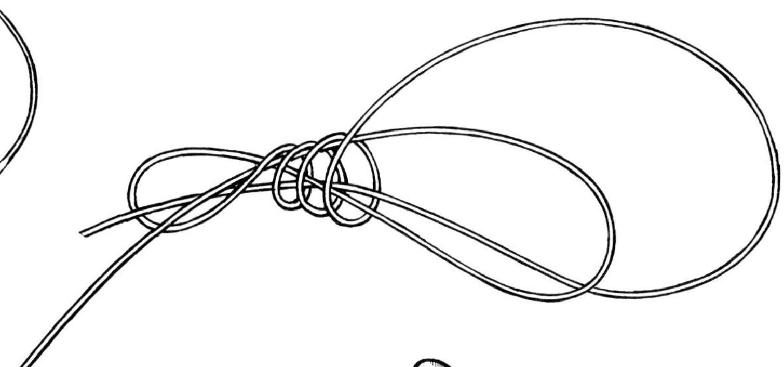

2. Wrap the small loop, the one you made first, with the larger loop.

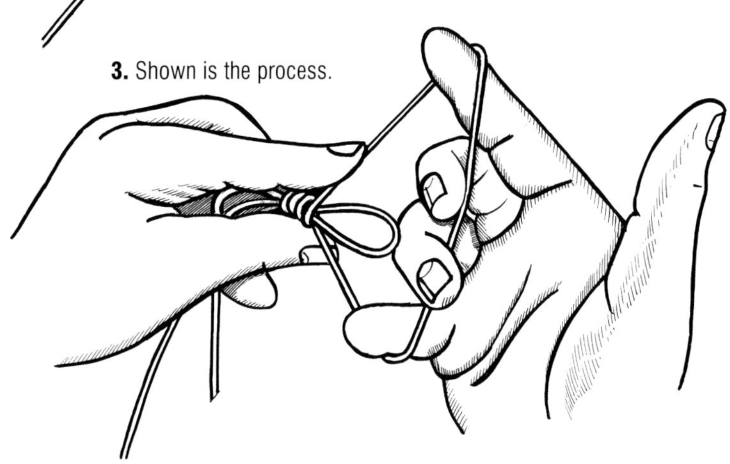

3. Shown is the process.

4. Continue until ten or a dozen wraps have been made.

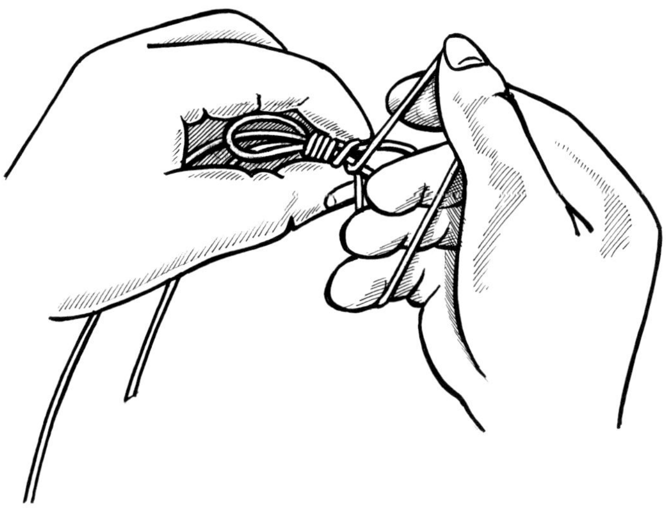

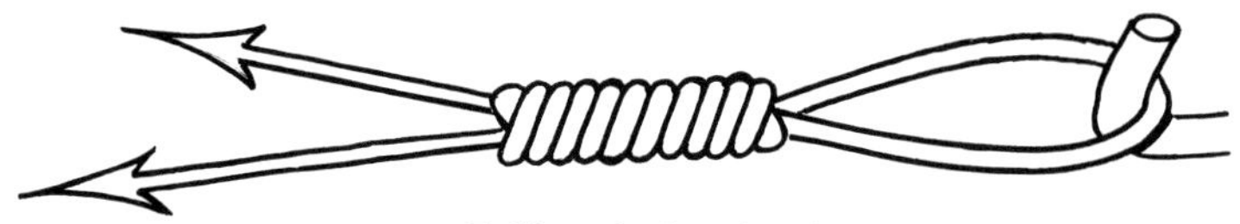

5. Close the knot but don't lock the knot in position because it has to slide.

6. Open the noose you have formed and slide it through the eye and over the point of the second hook. In this case a circle hook like I mostly use when tying this rig.

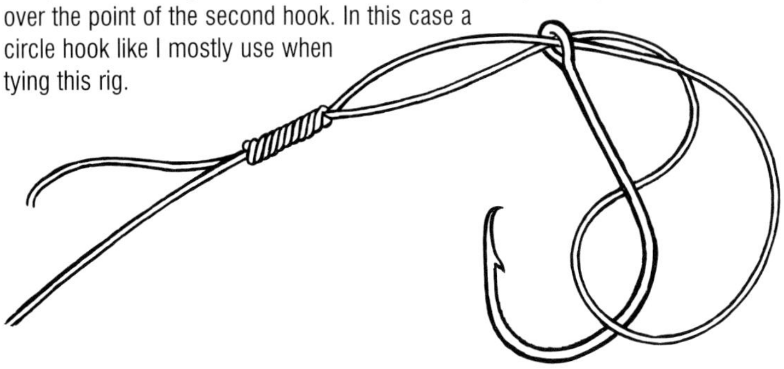

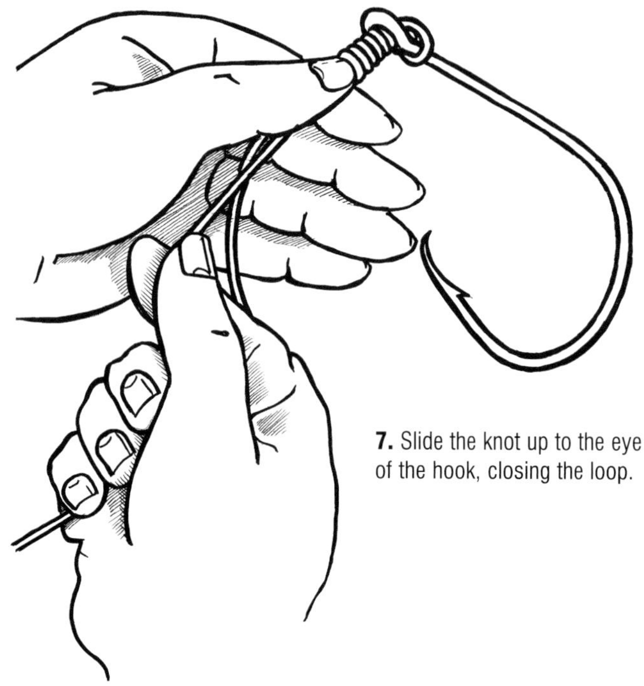

7. Slide the knot up to the eye of the hook, closing the loop.

8. To finish the knot, you will need to engage the hook with a rod holder or some fixed object so that you can pull back on the main line or leader to close the knot. Then, while maintaining pressure on the leader, take the tag and pull it until you feel the knot lock into place. The attachment of a circle hook in this orientation maximises it's hooking and holding potential

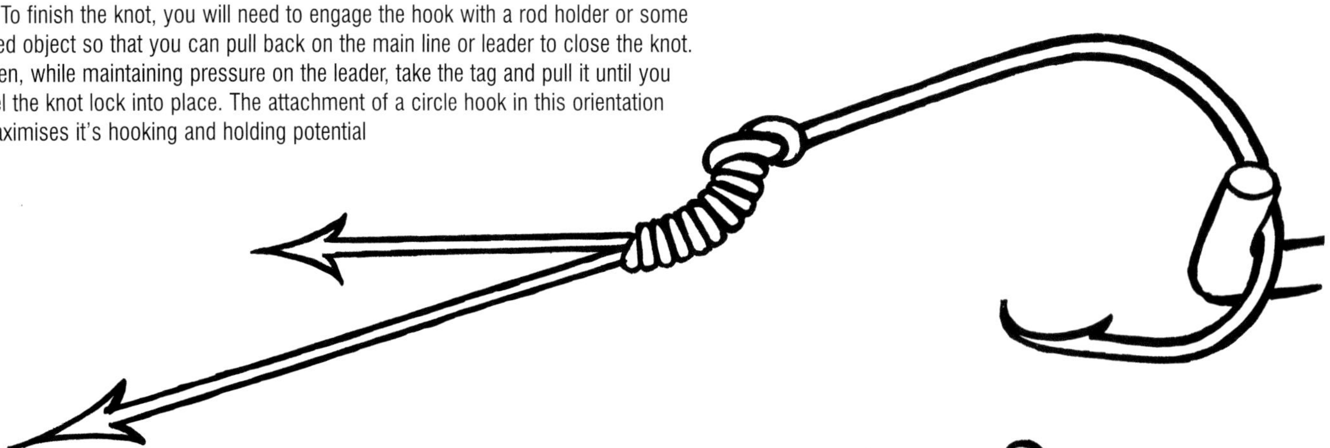

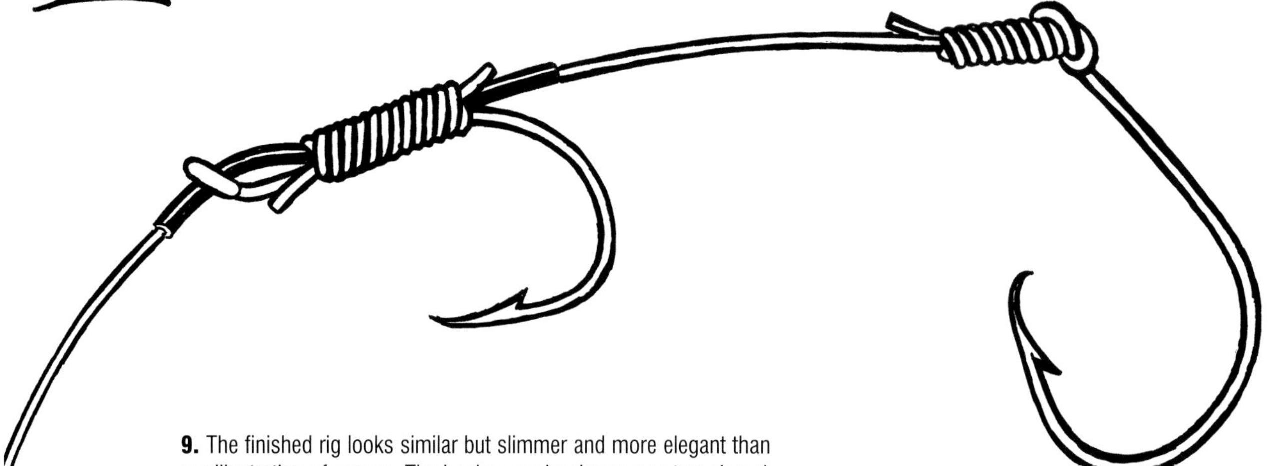

9. The finished rig looks similar but slimmer and more elegant than my illustration of course. The hooks may be drawn apart or closed together to accommodate baits of different sizes.

Chapter 6
PULLEY RIGS

Making Pulley Rigs

Pulley Rigs are used by serious beach fishermen and surf casters because their central strategy involves the use of some device that retains the baited hook behind the sinker until it hits the water, then releases it. This extends the distance of the cast and minimises overruns by preventing the baited hook and leader from flapping about.

Basically a pulley rig is constructed from length of line, heavier that than line coming from your reel and usually between say 5 to 10 feet (1.5 to 3 metres) long. There is a hook or hooks at one end and a sinker and release mechanism at the other, with a swivel – to which the line coming from your rod and reel is tied – in between. Two plastic beads, from say 0.2 to 0.3 inches (5 to 8 mm) in diameter are threaded onto the line either side of the swivel so it can't snare the knots at either end of the rig.

Basic Pulley Rig

On a basic pulley rig, the swivel to which the line from your rod and reel is tied, slides along the rig between the hook and the clip holding the sinker, buffered by the beads. When the hook is baited, then engaged with the release mechanism above the sinker to make the cast, a loop or doubled line is formed with the swivel at the apex so that a rig beginning with 6 feet (2 metres) of line is now less than 3 feet (a metre) in length.

This rig enables the angler to make an extended cast without getting the familiar backlash that's caused when an unsecured leader is free to flap about, and – if an efficient release mechanism is used – the baited hook is freed when the rig lands in the water.

Preventing Early Release with Large Baits

A problem I discovered with the basic pulley rig was that the use of too large a bait would cause the rig to fail and release prematurely because, relative to the sinker, large baits were simply too heavy and produced too much momentum of their own for the release mechanism to hold them.

The problem was solved simply by restricting the movement of the swivel on the rig (the one to which the line is tied) from free sliding, to being only allowed to slide under pressure. Presently I will show how this arrangement can be adjusted to allow one side of the rig (the hook length) to be shortened hold both the weight of the bait and sinker, while the opposite side of the rig (the sinker length) holds no weight and remains relatively slack.

Rigged like this you can cast out with a large bait untroubled by premature release, although you may have to adjust your rig before making the next cast.

Making an Advanced Pulley Rig

Materials:

• A 10 foot (3 metre) length of nylon monofilament about twice the breaking strain of your main line. That is to say if the line on your reel is 20 lb test (9 kg) then I suggest your rigging line should be about 40 lb test (18 kg).

• You will also require some heavier line (perhaps half as heavy again or about 60 lb (27 kg)). This is to tie a couple of nail knots with, and I'll explain more about that later.

• A large, strong swivel to act as the pulley.

• Two plastic beads for each rig, large enough (0.2 inches (5 mm)) so that they retain the swivel between them.

• Hooks of suitable size like the 4/0 and 6/0 used in making the two hook rig described previously in the chapter on adjustable hooks on page 28.

• Breakaway Impact Lead with wire tines for holding in side-drift and which also incorporates a release mechanism to engage then automatically disengage your baited hook or hooks.

• A short length of 1/16 inch (1.5 mm) inside diameter metal tubing for tying nail knots. I use the brass tubing made by K&S Engineering (http://www.ksmetals.com/) that you can buy from model aircraft component suppliers and some toy shops.

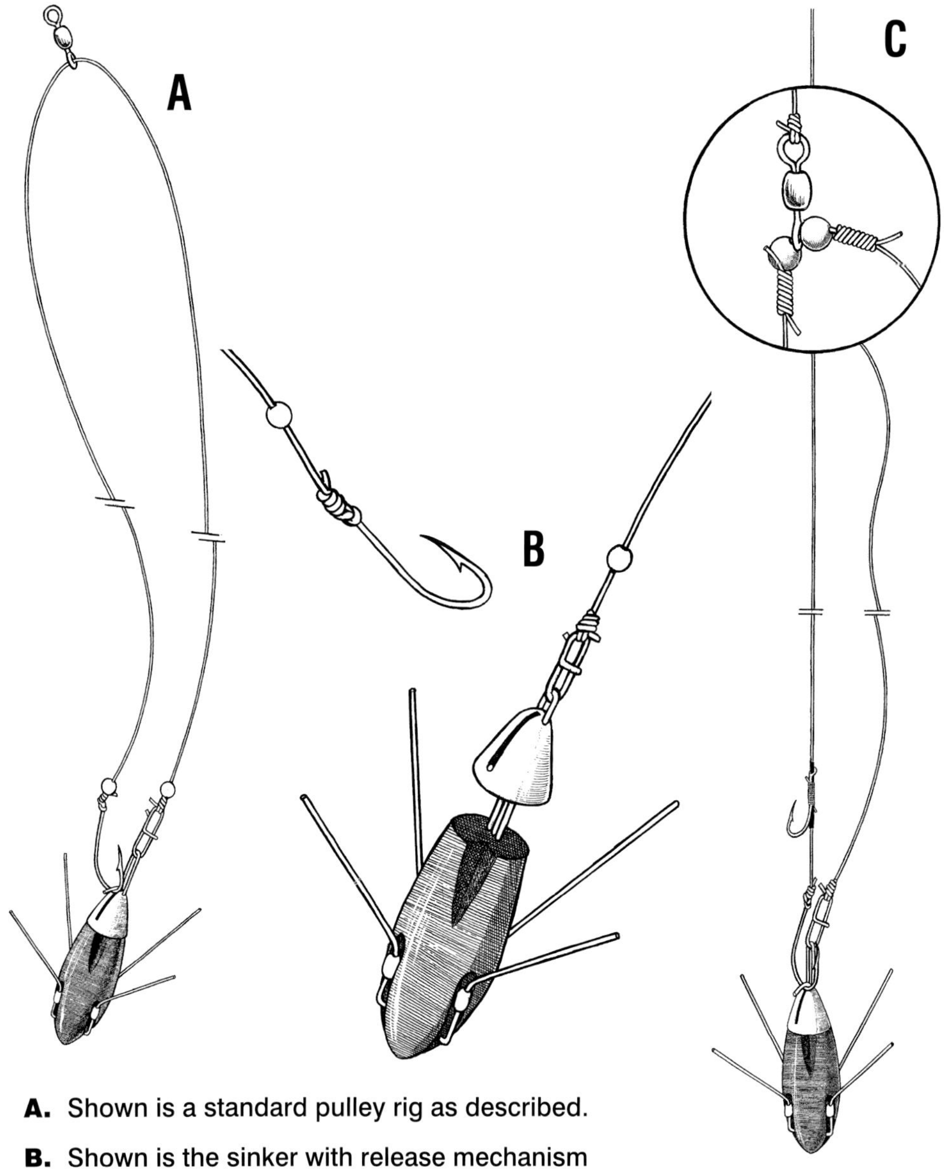

A. Shown is a standard pulley rig as described.

B. Shown is the sinker with release mechanism activated on impact with the water.

C. Shown again is the pulley rig in which two changes have been made:

- The rig now has two hooks rigged in a manner described in the section on rigging with multiple hooks so that a larger bait may be presented.
- The beads have now been slid right up against the swivel and temporarily held there by two nail knots, the same as we've previously described.

I say temporarily, because – unlike the previous nail knots that were tied in lighter line than the main line and were meant to be permanent fixtures on the line – these nail knots are not permanent fixtures on the line and must slide under pressure. It is for that that reason they are tied with heavier line. I suggest about half as heavy again as the construction line.

We also need another approach to tying these knots because there is no free end to encircle with the loop of tying line required in the previous method. Instead we use a slim brass tube (I use 1/64 inch (0.4 mm) inside diameter K&S brass tubing, or a Lumbar Puncture needle that you may be able to obtain from a surgical supplier).

I suppose that I should mention at this point that I have several nail-knotting tools that I've either purchased or been given by well-wishers, and my two little red Du Bro jobs have had plenty of use. Not so the others which have been unsatisfactory in one way or another. Besides, the metal tubes are cheaper to replace if you lose them.

Tying the Nail Knots

It is important to understand that when tying a nail knot as a permanent stopper on another line, the tying line – the one you are using to tie the nail knot with – should be lighter (preferably about half the breaking strain) than the line you are tying it to. This because the lighter line will lock down firmly on the main line and be – to all intents and purposes – permanent.

On the other hand, should we require the finished nail knot to slide along the line it is tied onto, but only under considerable pressure, we use line that is heavier and of greater diameter than the line onto which it is being tied.

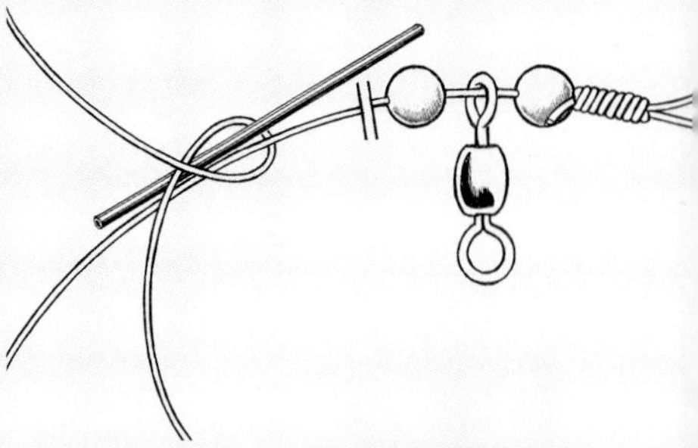

1. Shown is the first nail knot already tied in the heavier line, holding one of the two plastic beads in the mid section of the rig. As you can see the next nail knot is being tied in close proximity trapping the other bead, and the swivel, in between.

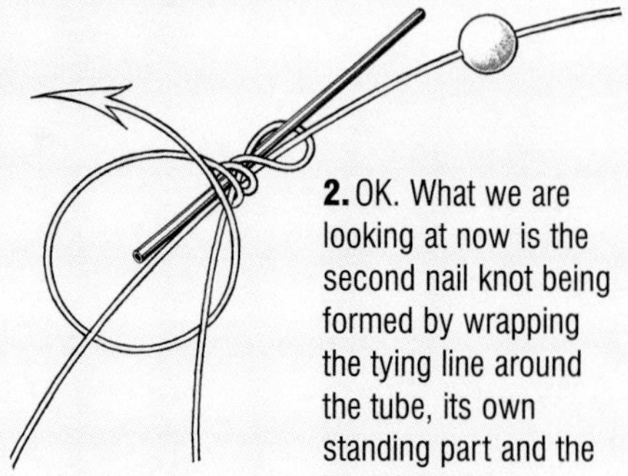

2. OK. What we are looking at now is the second nail knot being formed by wrapping the tying line around the tube, its own standing part and the line of the rig.

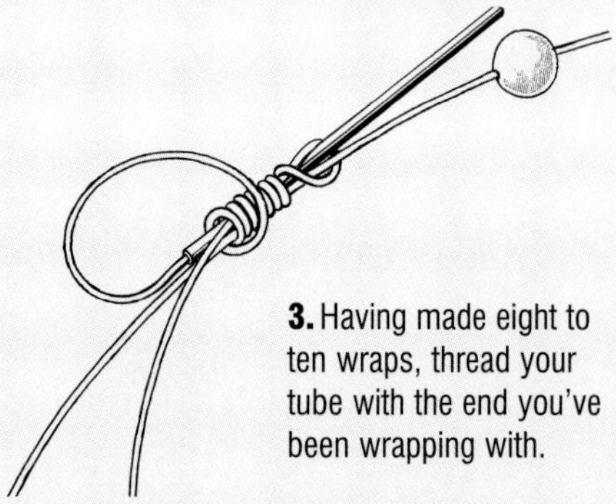

3. Having made eight to ten wraps, thread your tube with the end you've been wrapping with.

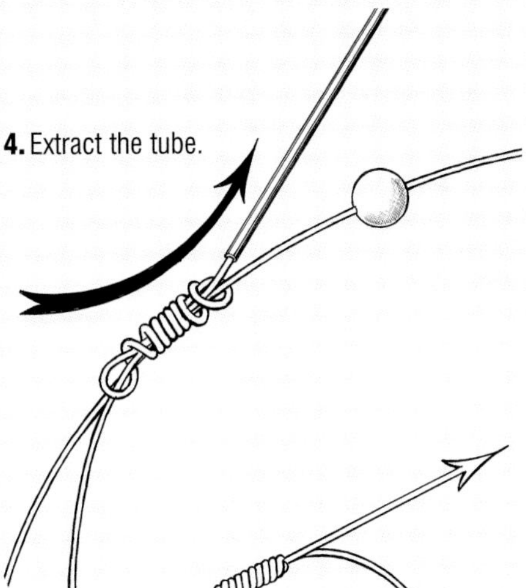

4. Extract the tube.

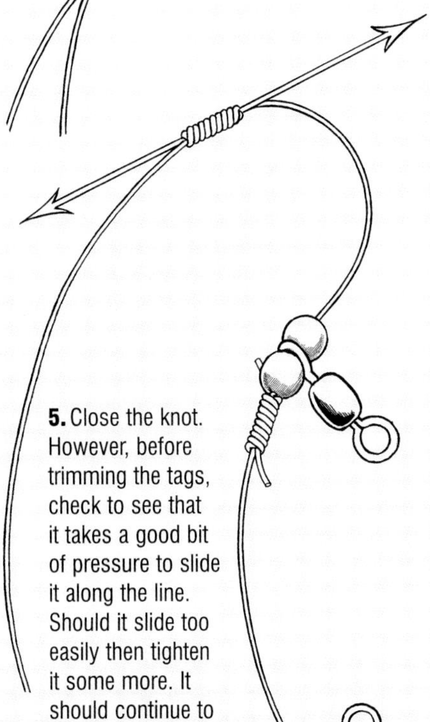

5. Close the knot. However, before trimming the tags, check to see that it takes a good bit of pressure to slide it along the line. Should it slide too easily then tighten it some more. It should continue to slide, but only under more pressure: It's a matter of judgement.

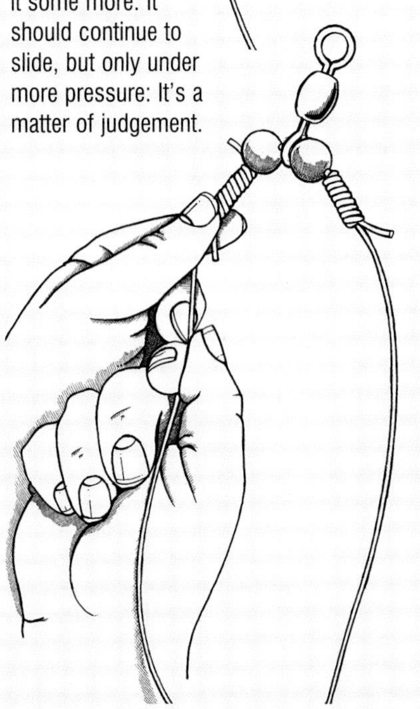

6. Slide the second nail knot up so that the swivel is the meat in the sandwich between the two beads and positioned so that the hook length is a bit shorter than the sinker length. This is so that when the rig is ready to be cast out, the weight of both the sinker and baited hooks are entirely supported by the hook length. This prevents the bait being released prematurely.

When rigged this way, on hooking any large fish, shark or ray, the swivel on the rig will slide back to the sinker end of the rig. This extends your hook length out to the full length of the rig, affording your lighter main line more protection, and shortening your previously 3 feet (a metre) long sinker length right up so that it is less likely to become snagged.

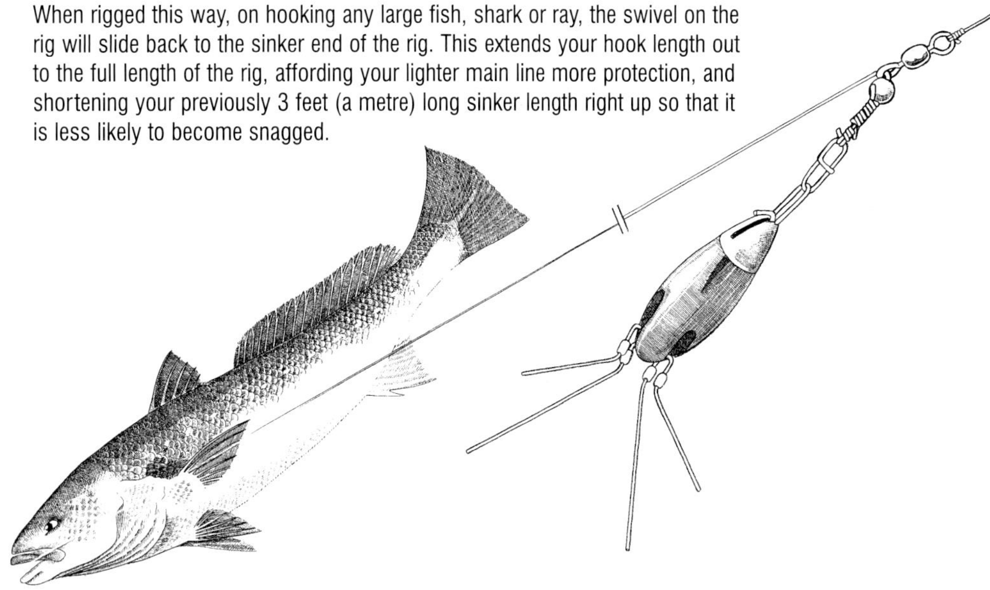

Other hook release devices

Having used a variety of hook releasing devices for pulley rigs, including a couple of my own design, which incidentally did not perform as well as hoped, I have used three devices that all work very well, and like the Breakaway Impact Lead we have already discussed the other two come from the Breakaway Tackle stable, and are worth some discussion.

Impact Shield

The Impact Shield is a small plastic device that can be threaded onto the rigging line, stabilized with a short length of rubber tubing and restrained between the clip holding the sinker and a bead and stopper combination. A bent arm slotted from top to bottom on the downward pointing side of the arm, holds the hook in place until the rig hits the water forcing the Impact Shield upwards, ejecting the hook.

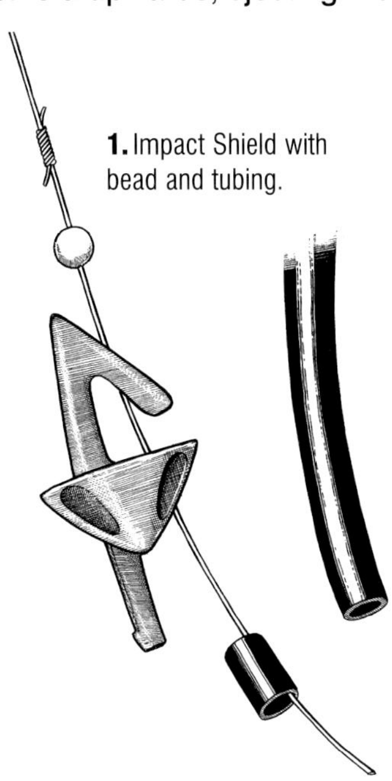

1. Impact Shield with bead and tubing.

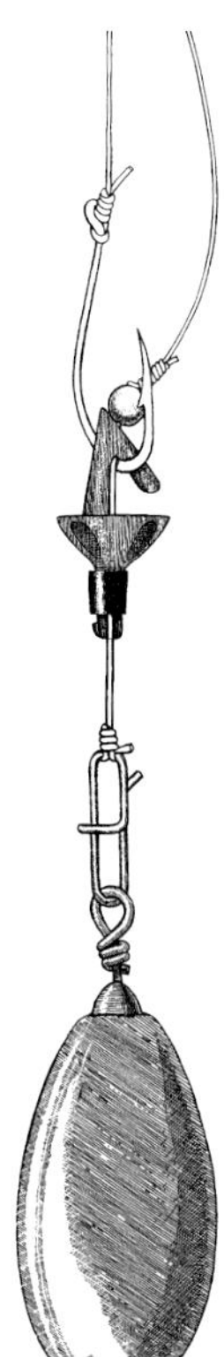

2. Shown is the Impact Shield rigged and ready to be cast out. Naturally the hook is baited.

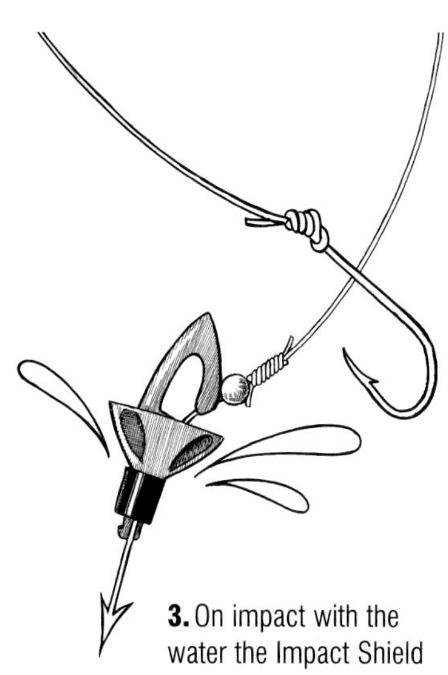

3. On impact with the water the Impact Shield is pushed sharply up against the bead and stopper, forcibly ejecting the hook.

Another alternative

Breakaway Fast links, the wire clips that facilitate the easy attachment of sinkers, swivels etc, those that I have been illustrating, may be used in conjunction with the Breakaway IMP release as a neat little unit.

Attaching one to the other is simple enough but I do advise the use of a coin, or like object, to open the fast link otherwise you may prick your thumb as many times as I did before I realized thls.

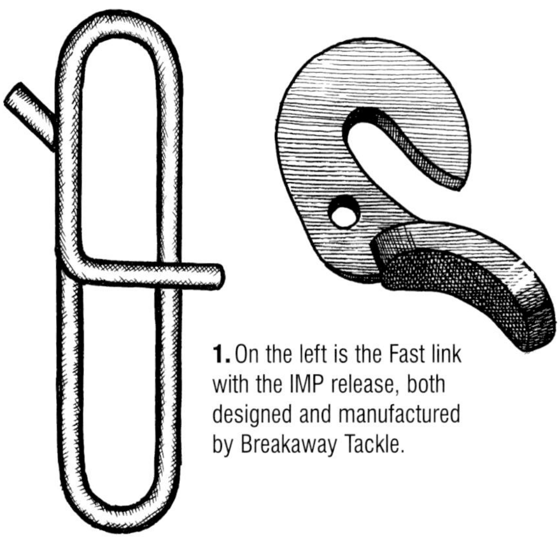

1. On the left is the Fast link with the IMP release, both designed and manufactured by Breakaway Tackle.

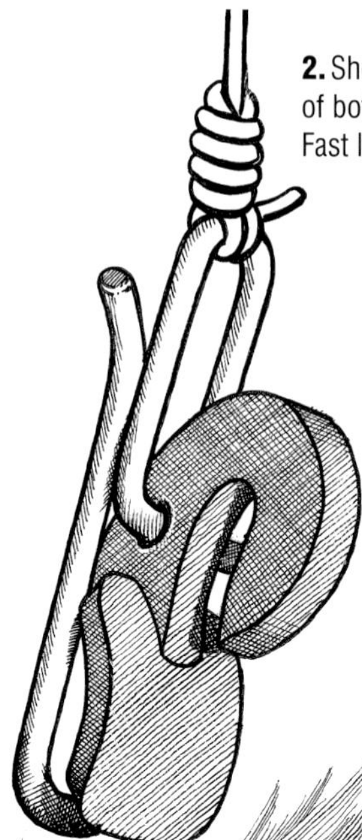

2. Shown is the marriage of both devices with the Fast link tied to the line.

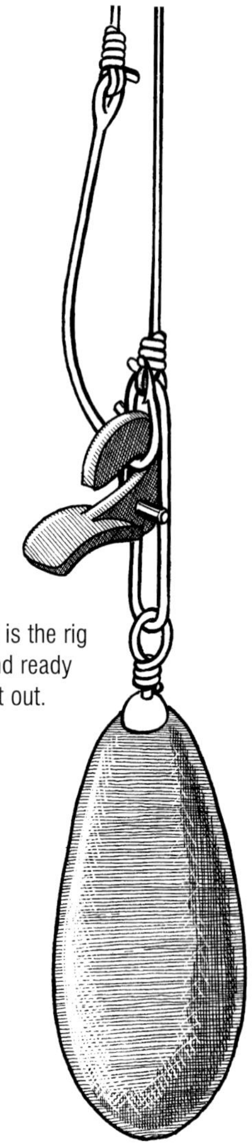

3. Shown is the rig loaded and ready to be cast out.

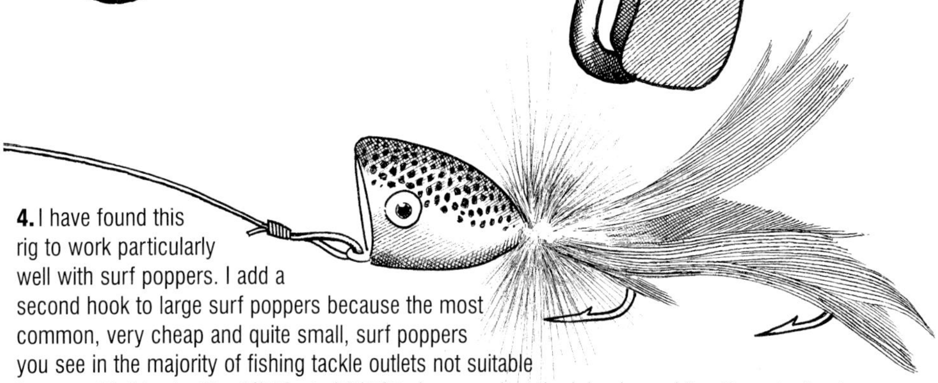

4. I have found this rig to work particularly well with surf poppers. I add a second hook to large surf poppers because the most common, very cheap and quite small, surf poppers you see in the majority of fishing tackle outlets not suitable for use with this rig. The 3/0 Mustad 91707s I use are just the job when adding the extra hook but any hook of the right size, and with a large enough eye, would probably do.

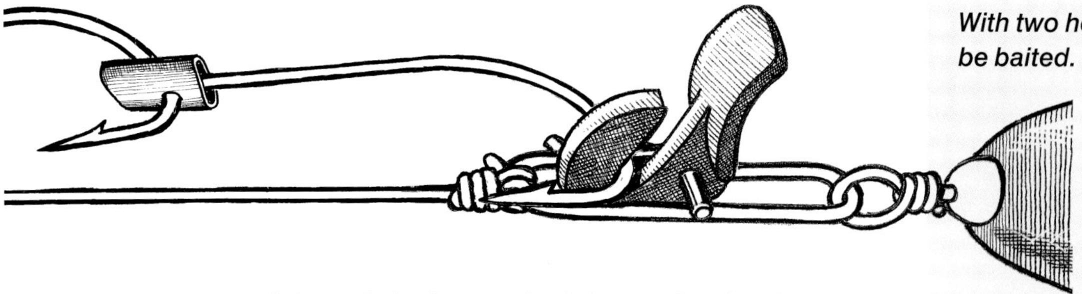

With two hooks on the popper it can be baited. In my experience though, the bait does not last very long if small fish are about. However, the popper remains working to and fro with the surge, sure to get the attention of any large fish attracted by the action of the bait thieves, and of course the remaining smell of bait on the popper. So don't be too quick to wind it back in after a bite or two that didn't hook up.

The great thing is that when fishing with a popper, snags are markedly reduced because the hooks remain buoyed up by the body of the popper.

5. This second hook can easily be attached to the popper by placing a small section of vinyl, plastic or hard rubber tubing over the eye of the second or trailing hook then threading the point of the hook on the popper through both the tubing and eye.

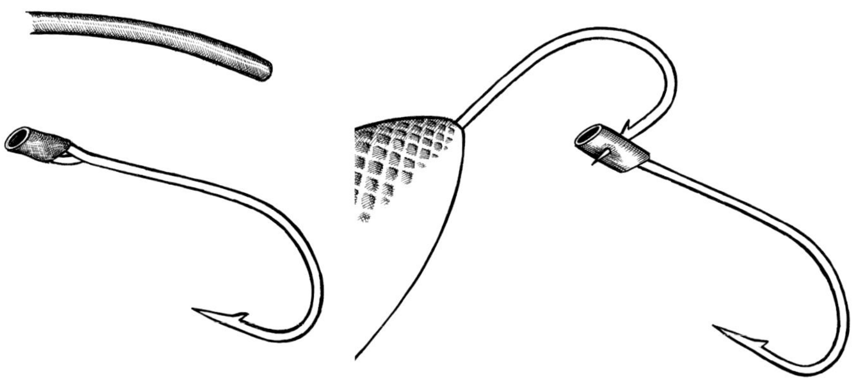

Baiting the Pulley Rig

Some consideration needs to be given to baiting the pulley rig because the dynamics of the cast could destroy or eject a bait that is not secure. In my use of the pulley rig I have used both slim strips of fish and squid bound to the hook and leader with bait elastic, which is available as Bait Mate or Ghost Cocoon in many fishing tackle stores.

I initially encountered some problems when using whole fish that were overcome by the use of a small electrical cable tie in the manner shown.

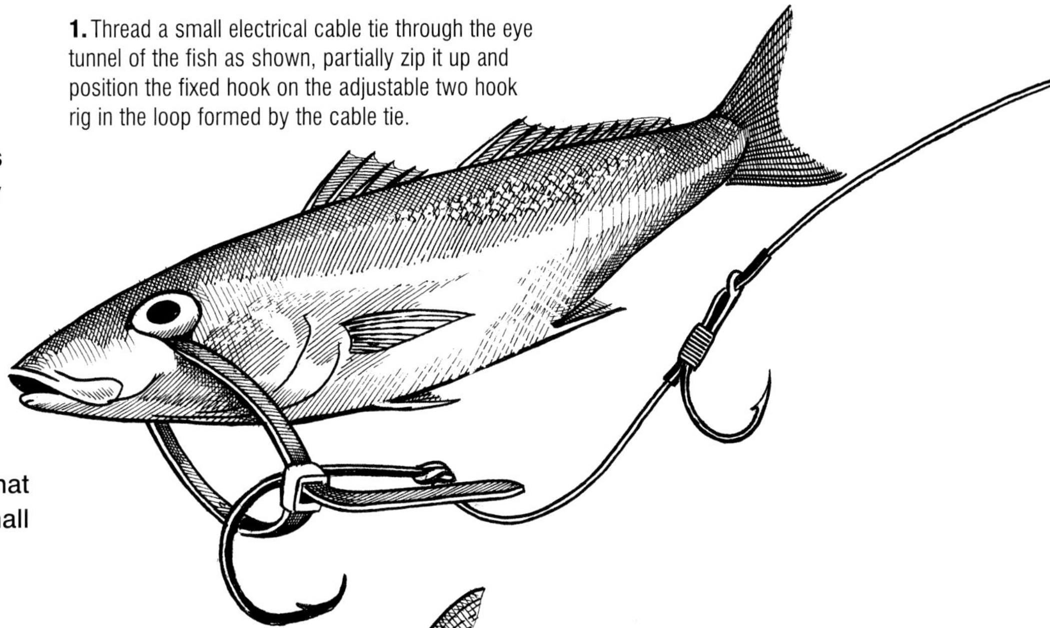

1. Thread a small electrical cable tie through the eye tunnel of the fish as shown, partially zip it up and position the fixed hook on the adjustable two hook rig in the loop formed by the cable tie.

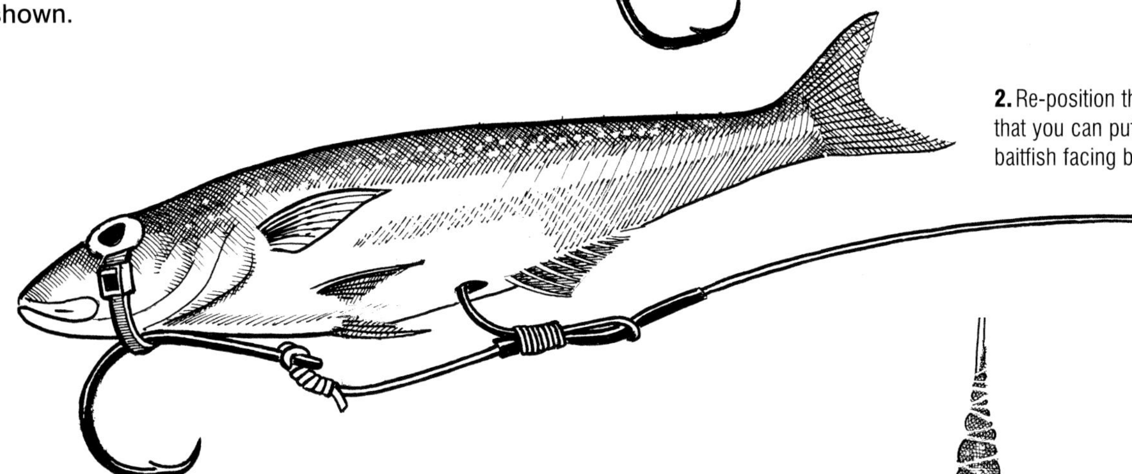

2. Re-position the sliding hook so that you can put it in the anus of the baitfish facing backwards.

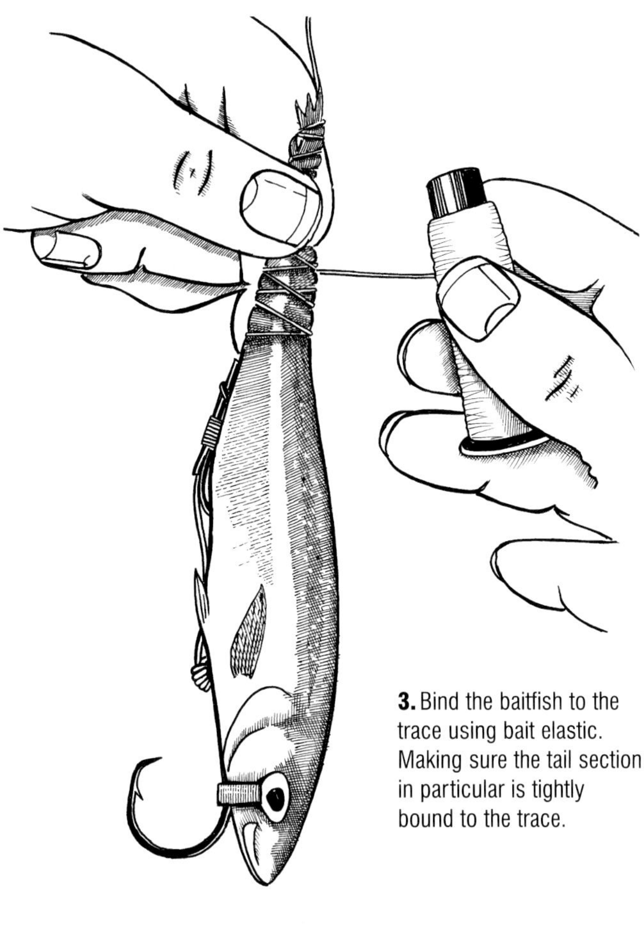

3. Bind the baitfish to the trace using bait elastic. Making sure the tail section in particular is tightly bound to the trace.

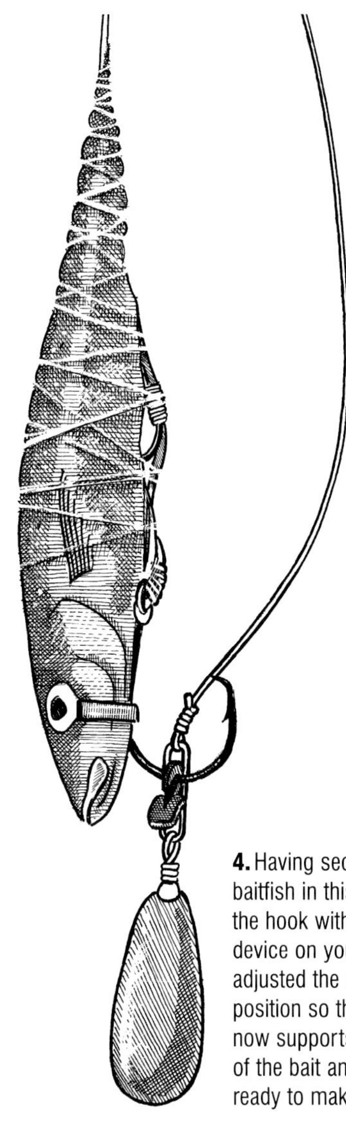

4. Having secured your whole baitfish in this way, engaging the hook with the release device on your rig, and adjusted the swivel (pulley) position so the hook length now supports both the weight of the bait and sinker, you are ready to make a cast.

Chapter 7 GELSPUN LINES

Advanced Rigging with Gelspun Lines

The diversity and composition of the various gelspun lines on the market, both braided and fused, all inappropriately referred to as "Braid," makes it difficult to generalize rigging procedures, leave alone estimate what percentage of the line's breaking strain is retained when any particular knot or splice is used.

When I say inappropriately referred to as "Braid" I should point out that the first braided gelspun lines were woven on the very same weaving looms used to make braided nylon, braided dacron etc. Besides, some gelspun lines are constructed from fused parallel fibres and are not braided in any way, so referring to those as "Braid" is nonsense.

As anyone in the business of testing lines would readily affirm, some gelspun lines test way, way over; two or three times and more, of what the packaging on the spool indicates, while others test substantially less than what is marked. Few, if any, are marked with actual line tests.

Only if required

For the majority of those who use gelspun lines for casting and retrieving lures for fish that are considerably lighter than the stated breaking strain, leave alone the tested breaking strain of the line, this is of little concern, and – given that many gelspun lines break well over what is stated on the spool – there is rarely going to be a problem using low yield knots.

However, should your intention be to seriously target large and powerful fish on gelspun lines through deep water jigging, offshore trolling, surf fishing, or through live or dead bait fishing, the imperative to retain as much as the line's breaking strain as possible becomes abundantly clear.

Having produced a double, the doubled strand or loop may then be tied off to a nylon or fluorocarbon monofilament leader, looped leader splice, or metal fixture such as a clip or swivel. In doing this you will retain the as much of the line's strength as possible.

Trying a double

There are two approaches that I know of that produce high strength doubles in both gelspun and monofilament lines; they are the Plait and the Bimini twist. The plait takes longer to produce but it's a powerful tool when creating joins between gelspun lines and attaching leaders.

On the other hand a Bimini double or end loop is reasonably easy to produce but the technique of tying a Bimini in gelspun line is somewhat stricter than with monofilament, but more on that as we go along.

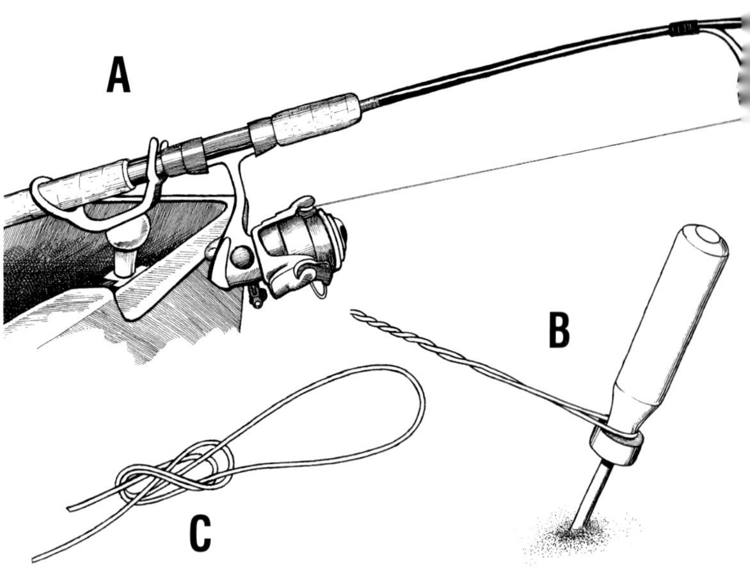

Bimini Twist (*Bimini Double*)

A. Your rod and reel, or spool of line, may be held by another person who can keep the line tight for you; or your rod and reel may be placed in a rod holder so that tension may be maintained on the line.

B. You will need a fixed point, as represented by this large screw-driver I've hammered into the ground, as the second tensioning point. Your fixed point may be anything from another rod holder in your boat to the garden tap, depending on location.

C. Tie a loop in the end of your gelspun line and put aside to use as a pull through to finish of your Bimini double.

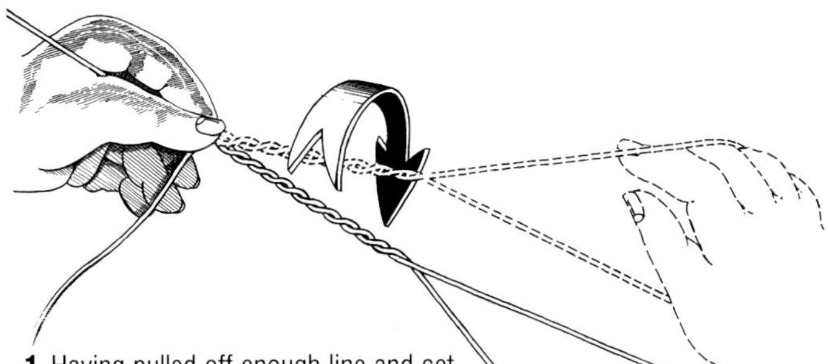

1. Having pulled off enough line and set the drag on your reel to maximum for the line size you are using, make a loop with a very generous tag and roll in as many twists as required. I don't go beyond fifty twists because of the extra wear and tear on the line caused by the rotation of your hand and the tendency for the line to kink with additional twists.

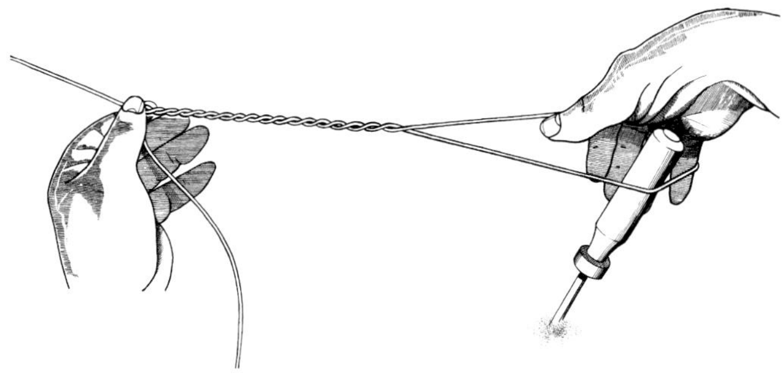

2. Having set the drag on your reel to maximum for the line you are using, and rolled in the required number of twists, fifty say, place the loop over your fixed point, holding the tag of the line so that it doesn't unravel.

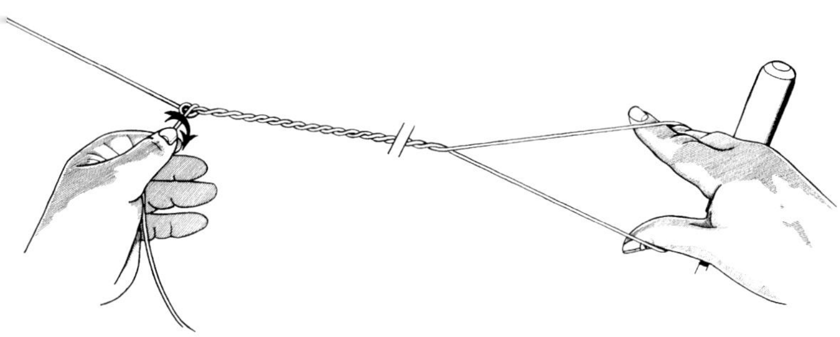

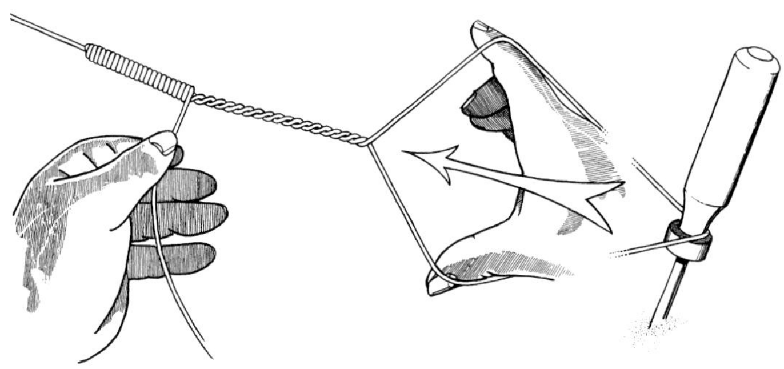

3. What you see here is a representation of how the Bimini is formed. You will see that the thumb and finger of the left hand rotate the tag (clockwise in this case) to initiate its roll-back while the right hand compresses the twists from the other end.

Please be aware that compressing the twists from the top or tag end as some do by pulling the tag and main line apart with the loop around their feet and knees, is fatal to gelspun lines and has lead to misleading conclusions by some well meaning folk about the value of the Bimini for gelspun and how many turns are optimal when tying a Bimini in gelspun line.

4. Continue to compress the twists while guiding the tag's roll-back over the twists ...

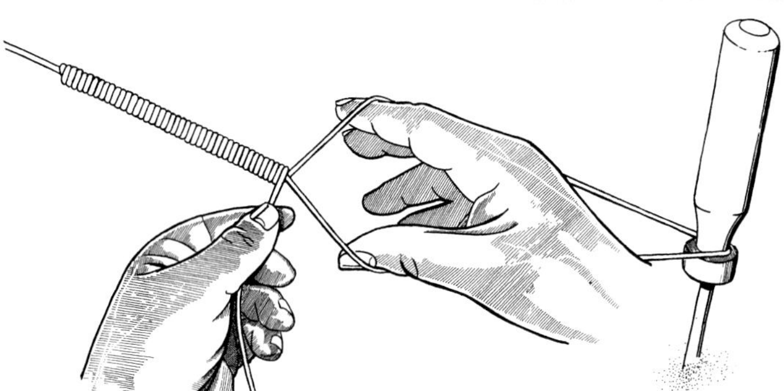

5. Until the tag is right up to the crotch in the loop.

6. Introduce the small loop you formed at the beginning in diagram C, wrap it with the tag from say four to six times, then thread it with the tag. Wrap it tightly of course, I have opened up the wraps and removed the hands so that you can clearly see what is happening.

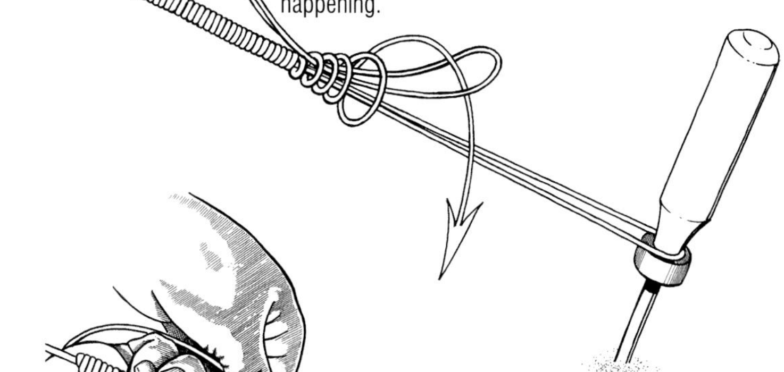

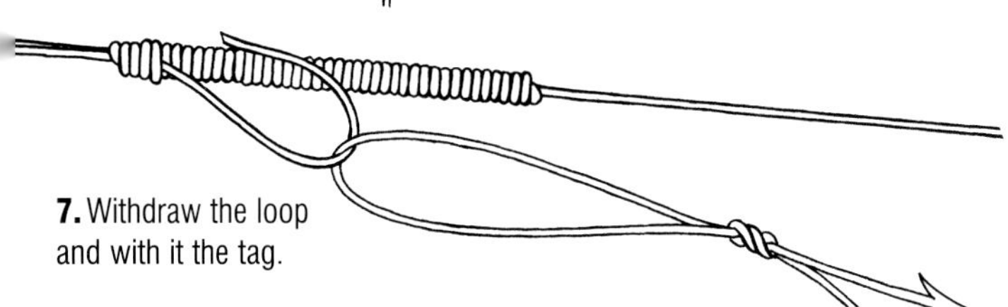

7. Withdraw the loop and with it the tag.

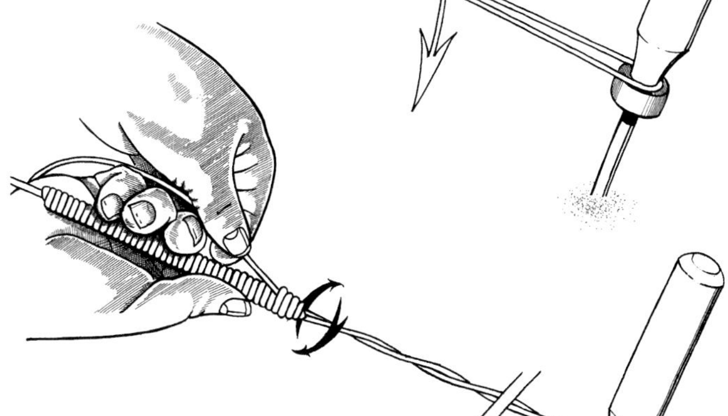

Please be aware that this is a powerful finish that really locks the Bimini down far more securely than half hitching. However, if you zip it up too tight the tag will shear off, and – because the point of shear on the tag is uncertain – you will need to tie it again.

8. You may need an assistant to re-tension your line by winding up the reel a bit at this stage because the line must be really tight. With one hand, rotate the Bimini as shown by the rotational arrows then with the other hand pull back on the tag until you feel the last few turns zip up really tight. The line must be really tight for this to happen

Making Connections with the Bimini Cat's Paw to Clip

I use the Cat's Paw when fishing in the surf because it enables the attachment and removal of a wire snap or open-plan snap without having to re-tie the Bimini each time I go fishing. Let's take a closer look at that.

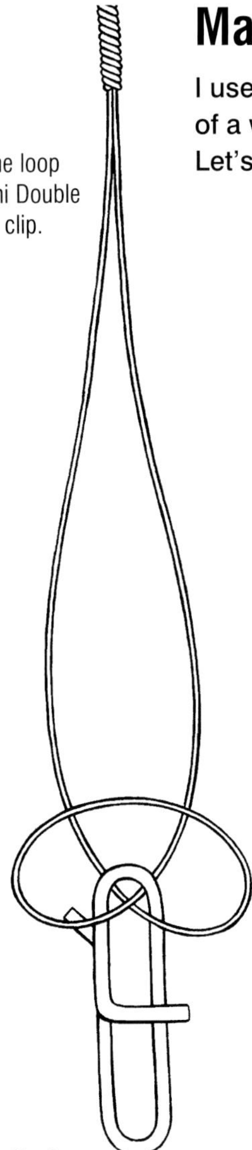

1. Thread the loop of the Bimini Double through the clip.

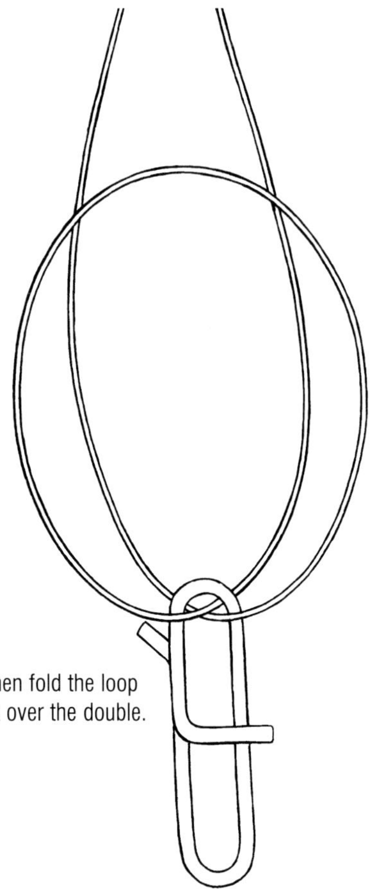

2. Then fold the loop back over the double.

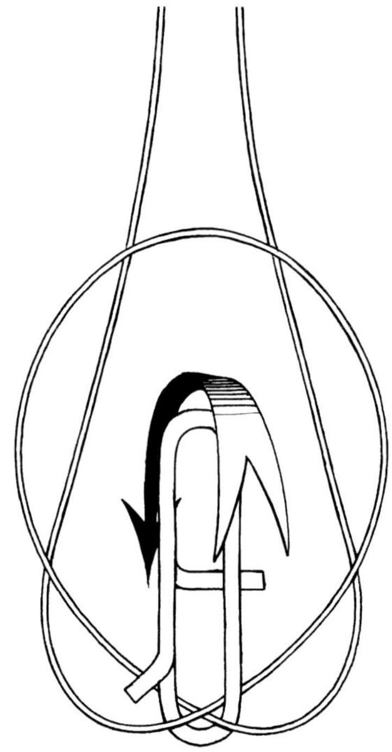

3. Rotate the clip through the loop.

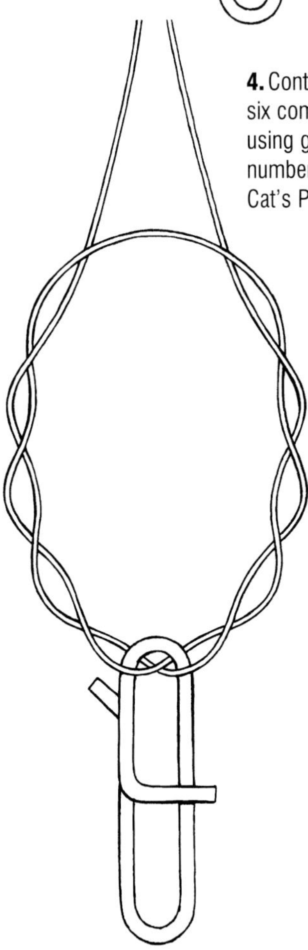

4. Continue until you have made six complete rotations when using gelspun line, half that number should you be tying a Cat's Paw in monofilament.

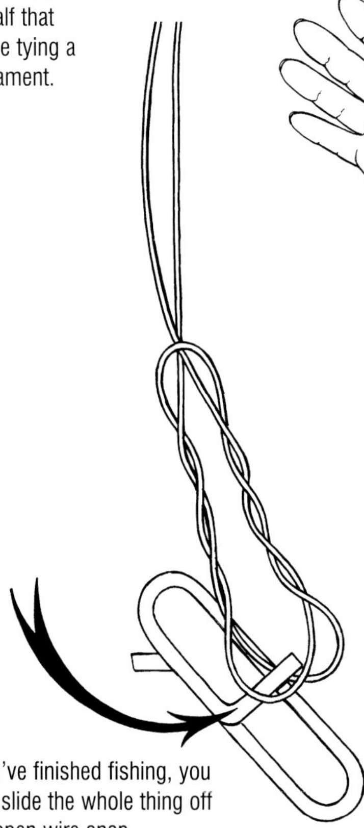

5. After you've finished fishing, you can simply slide the whole thing off the clip or open wire snap.

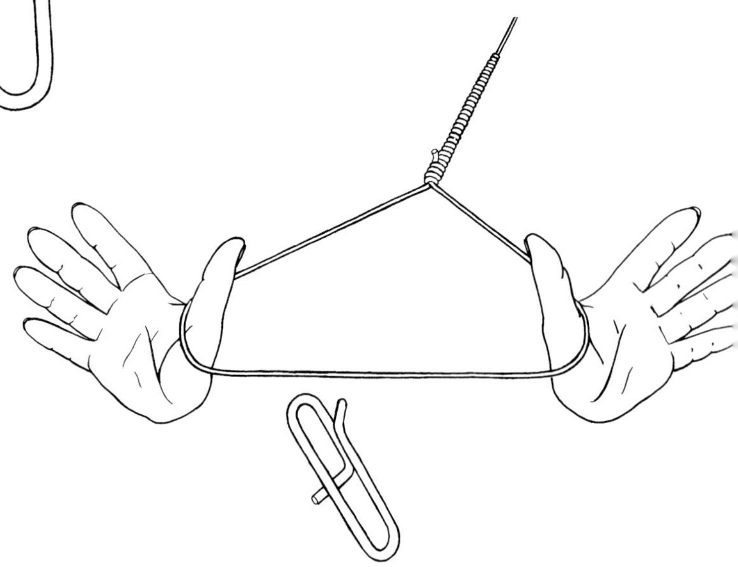

6. Having removed the Cat's Paw from the clip you can just open out the Bimini Loop and wind it back through the rod guides and onto your reel ready for next time. It saves you re-tying the Bimini each time you go fishing.

Naturally, there will be a certain amount of wear and tear and this is cumulative; so fishing for days on end without retying the Bimini will eventually result in snapping off the rig when you cast out. I know because it's happened to me once or twice through being lazy.

Joining Gelspun Lines

There are two sound ways of joining gelspun lines, both of which can be easily verified with a set of scales. They are the Bimini Cat's Paw Splice and the Plaited Splice.

Bimini Cat's Paw Splice

When replacing the worn section of your line, which could range from 330 feet (100 metres) with surf fishing tackle, down to 60 feet (18 metres) when lure casting with light tackle, it's a good idea to sacrifice as little of your line's breaking strain as possible. This is done by tying a Bimini Double in both the line on your reel, and the line that you are replacing the worn section with.

As we have previously discussed, your rod and reel can be placed in a rod holder which makes tying the Bimini Double possible with a single person. However, because your replacement line is on a plastic spool you will need to have someone hold the spool and tension the line as directed.

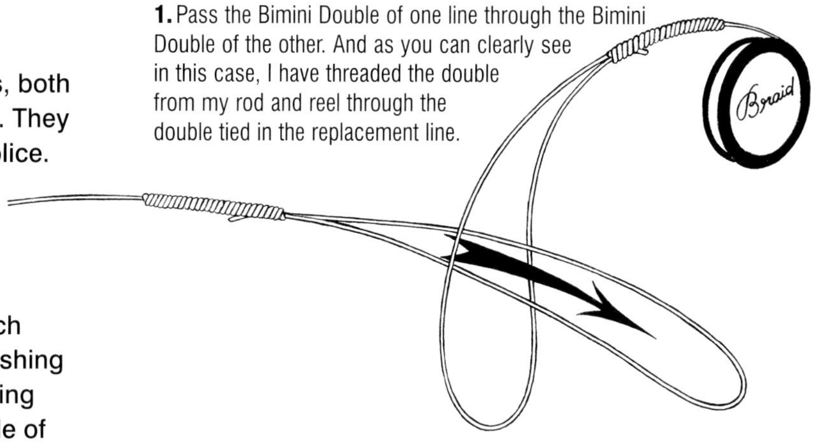

1. Pass the Bimini Double of one line through the Bimini Double of the other. And as you can clearly see in this case, I have threaded the double from my rod and reel through the double tied in the replacement line.

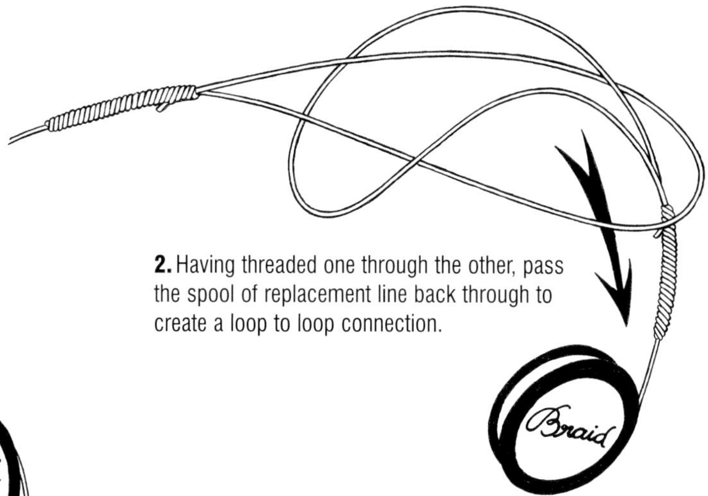

2. Having threaded one through the other, pass the spool of replacement line back through to create a loop to loop connection.

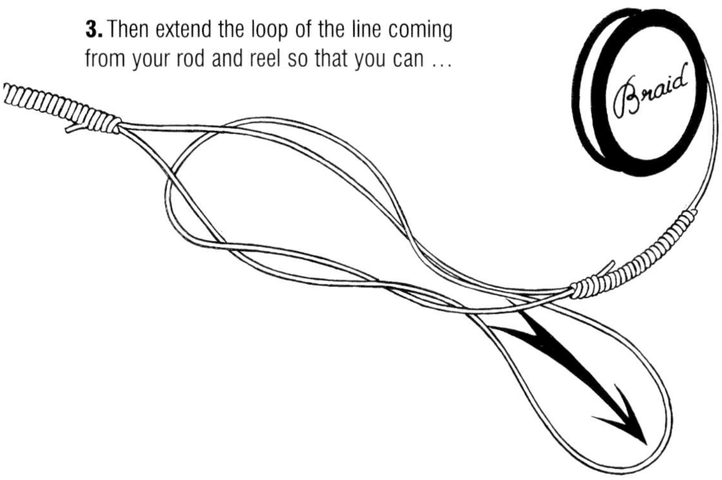

3. Then extend the loop of the line coming from your rod and reel so that you can …

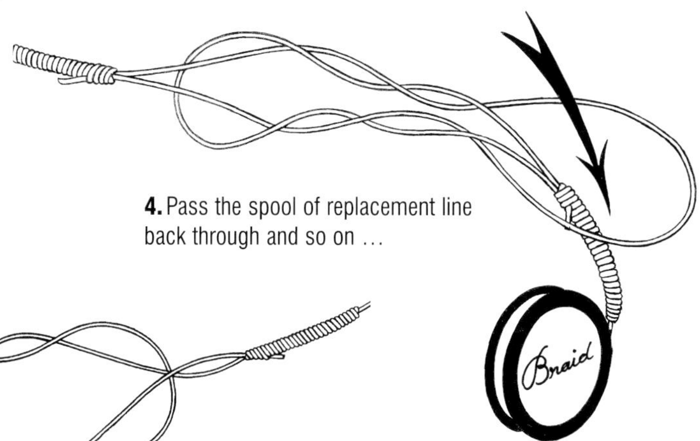

4. Pass the spool of replacement line back through and so on …

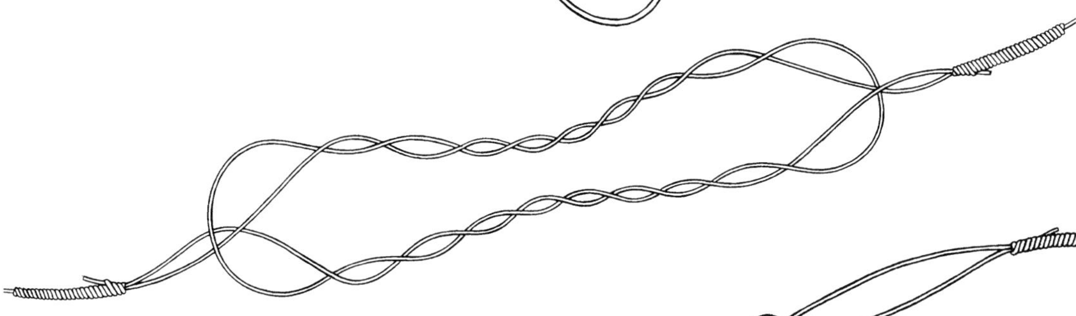

5. Until you have made ten wraps.

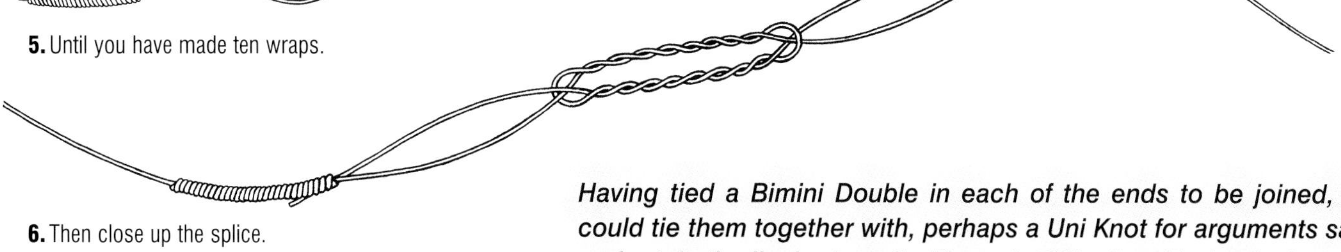

6. Then close up the splice.

Having tied a Bimini Double in each of the ends to be joined, you could tie them together with, perhaps a Uni Knot for arguments sake, and retain the line's strength. The only difficulty with that is that, with two strands being tied together in each line, the knot becomes bulky.

The Cat's Paw is a very slim and unobtrusive join and retains a very high percentage of the line's strength.

Attaching a Leader using a Bimini Twist Double and Plaited Splice

Having tied a Bimini or plaited double in your line you are almost ready to add a nylon or fluorocarbon monofilament leader, or – should you prefer – a heavier gelspun leader as I have done on occasion.

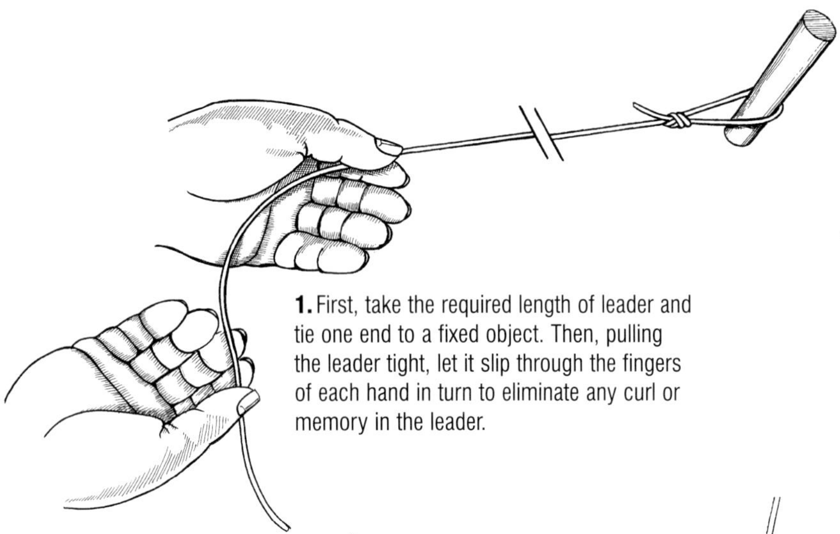

1. First, take the required length of leader and tie one end to a fixed object. Then, pulling the leader tight, let it slip through the fingers of each hand in turn to eliminate any curl or memory in the leader.

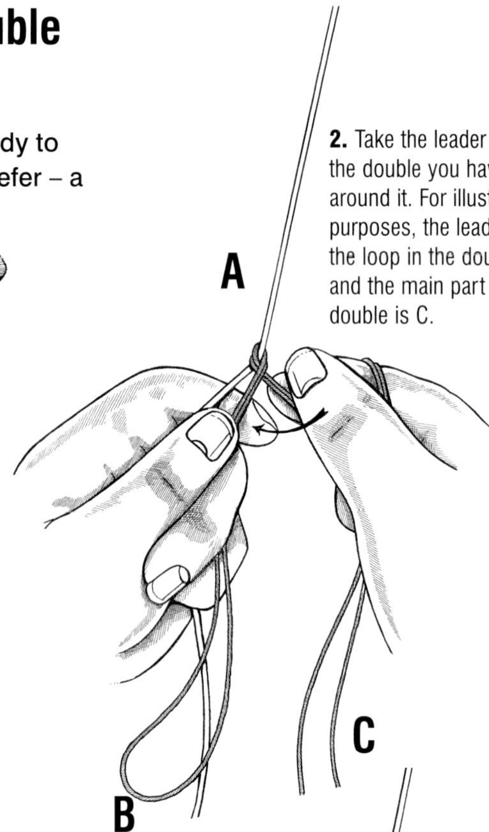

2. Take the leader and wrap the double you have tied, around it. For illustrative purposes, the leader is A, the loop in the double is B, and the main part of the double is C.

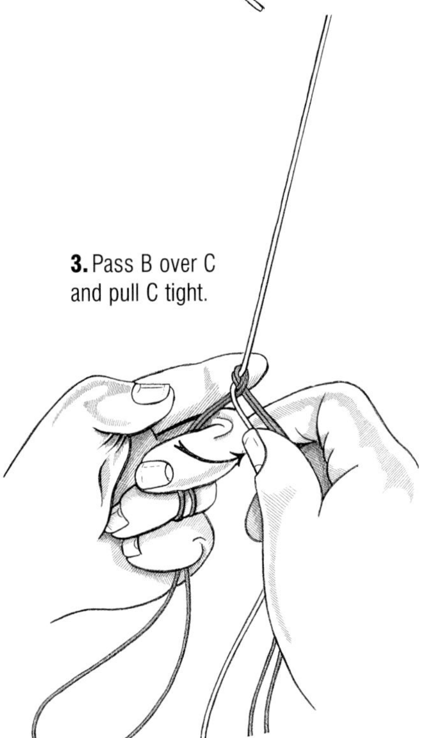

3. Pass B over C and pull C tight.

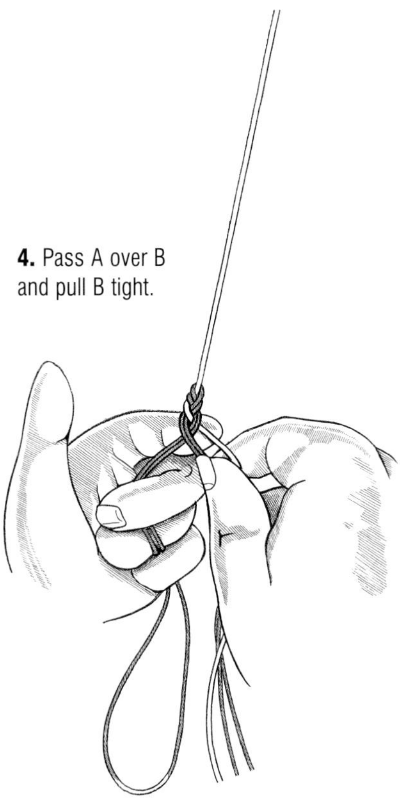

4. Pass A over B and pull B tight.

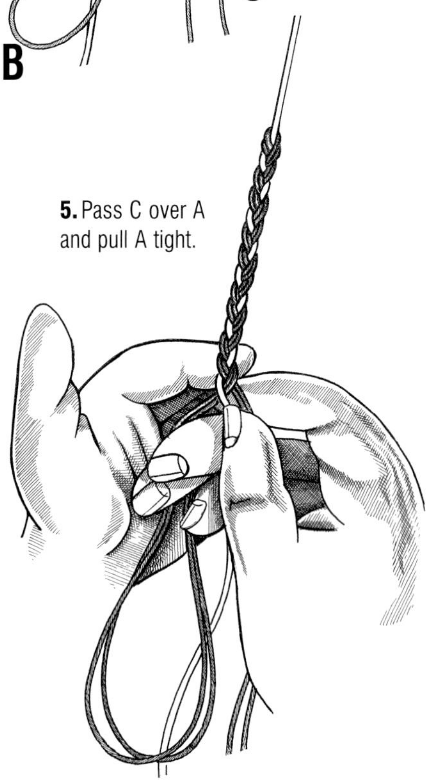

5. Pass C over A and pull A tight.

6. And so on passing the left and right legs alternatively to the centre until you have plaited at least one inch (2.5 mm) for every 10 lb (4.5 kg) of your lighter line.

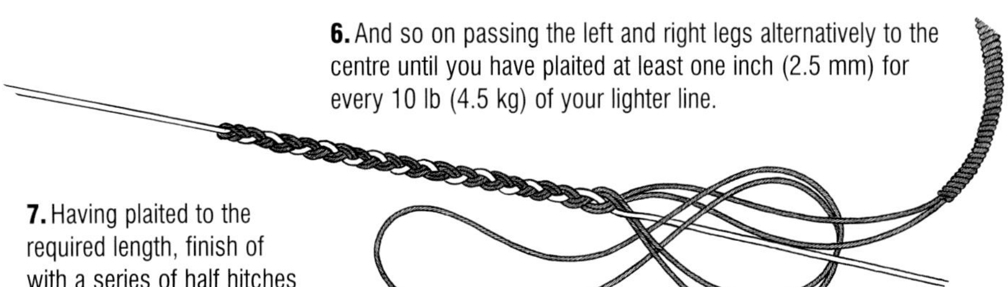

7. Having plaited to the required length, finish of with a series of half hitches with the residual loop around both the leader tag and the double.

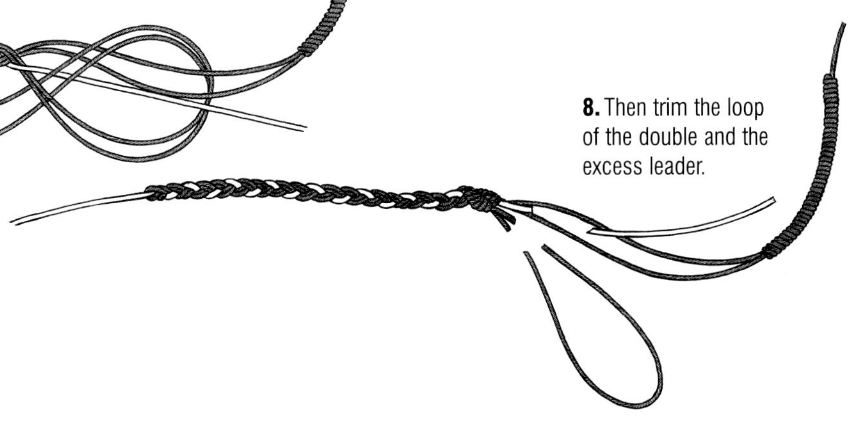

8. Then trim the loop of the double and the excess leader.

Because the leader is not folded over or tied, this full-strength splice remains slim and unobtrusive.

Single Strand Gelspun to Leader using the Plaited Splice

The Plaited Splice is sometimes used to attach leaders to a single strand of gelspun and it does make a sound connection although not as strong as strong as claimed by at least some of its proponents.

For the purposes of this illustration the monofilament leader is A, The main line is C and the tag is B. Make sure the tag B is long enough. I made it appear shorter in my illustration so that it doesn't become confused with C.

1. Having secured the opposite end of your leader as we did when plaiting with the Bimini Double, and straightened it out with your fingers to remove the curl or memory, wrap your mono leader with the gelspun line as shown.

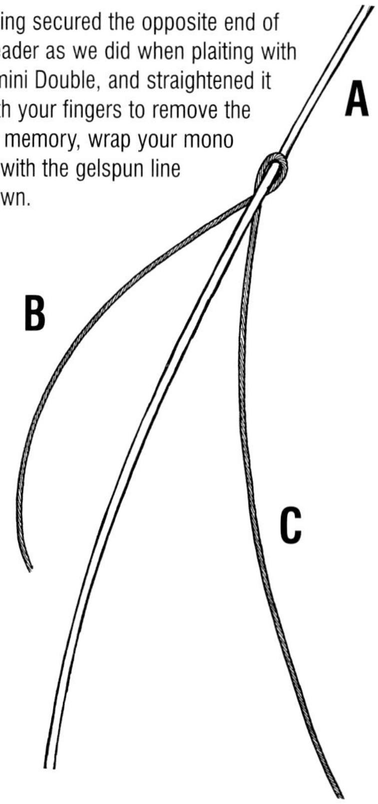

2. Pass B over A while maintaining tension on A.

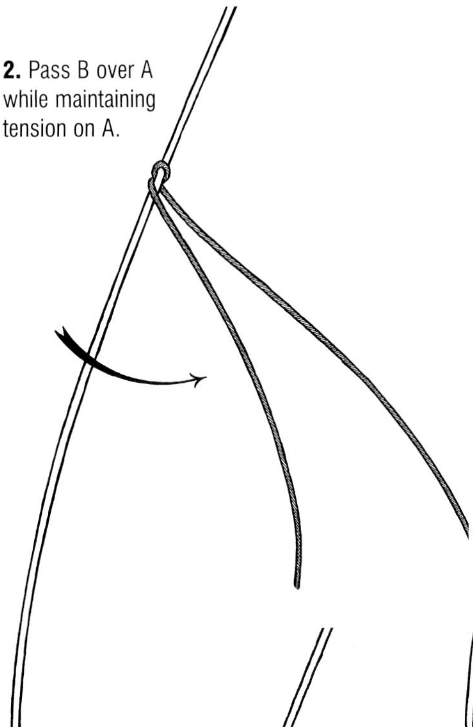

3. Pass C over B and tension B.

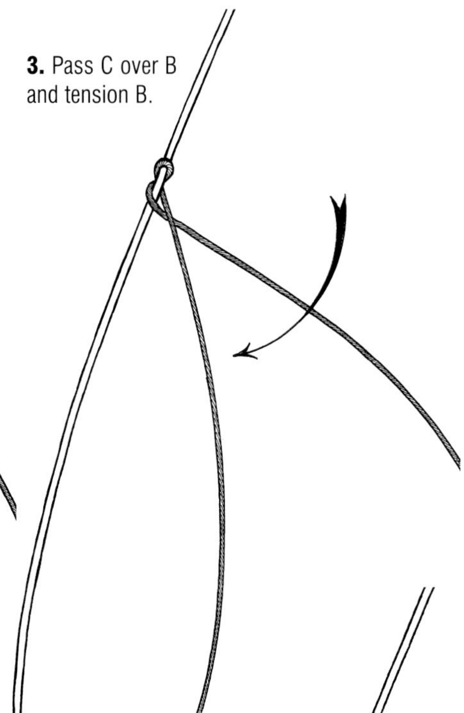

4. Pass A over C and tension C.

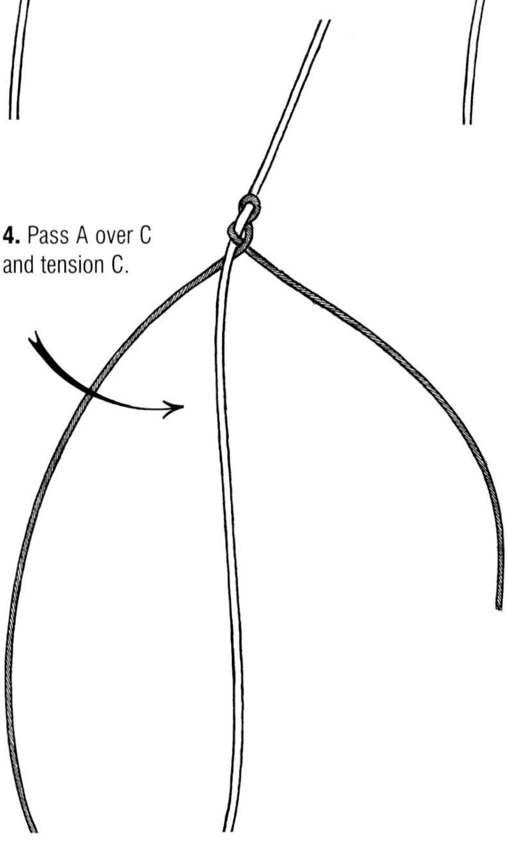

5. Pass B over A and tension A.

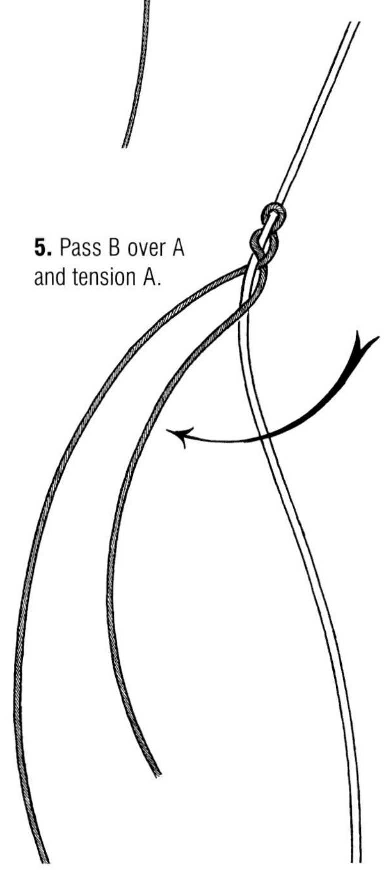

6. And so on until you have plaited at least an inch for every 10 lb (4.5 kg) breaking of your line then finishing off with a series of half hitches as before, trimming off the gelspun tag and excess leader.

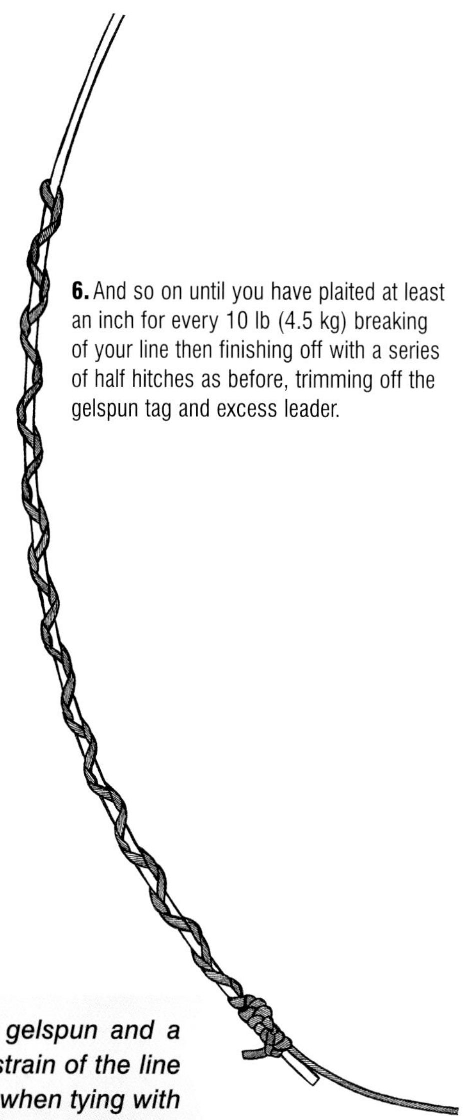

While this join provides a sound connection between a single strand of gelspun and a monofilament leader, and may indeed test at or above the stated breaking strain of the line you are using, it is in no way comparable in strength to the same join made when tying with a properly configured Bimini or Plaited Double: How could it be?

Top Shotting (replacing worn line) with the Plaited Splice

Replacing the top 60 to 330 feet (18 to 100 metres) or more of line on your reel with new line after an extended period of use is a good idea whether you are using gelspun or monofilament.

We've already looked at doing so with the Bimini Cat's Paw Splice, now we are going to look at doing so with the plaited spice. You probably have the idea by now but it won't hurt to have another look at the process using two similar, but in this case, two differently coloured lines, one dark and one light so you can clearly see the procedure.

1. Place your rod and reel in a secure rod holder and thread the guides. The line coming from the rod and reel is dark in colour and marked A. The line that you are attaching is light in colour so you can follow. The main or standing part of the new line is C and the returning end or tag is B.

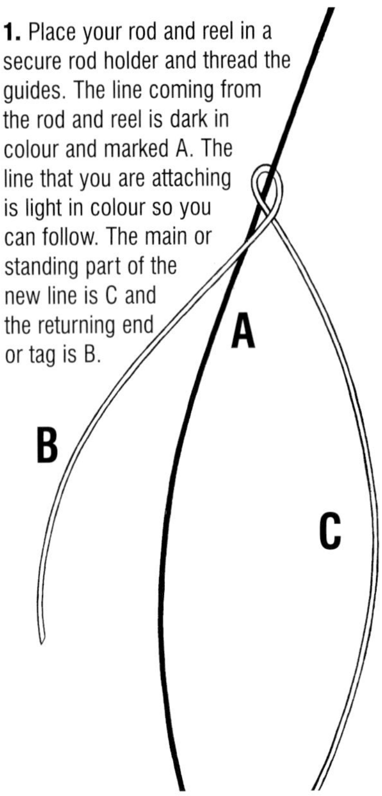

2. What you've seen so far should enable the following sequence. In this illustration I have opened the Plait so you can see the configuration clearly. Of course you will be Plaiting under tension and it won't be open like that.

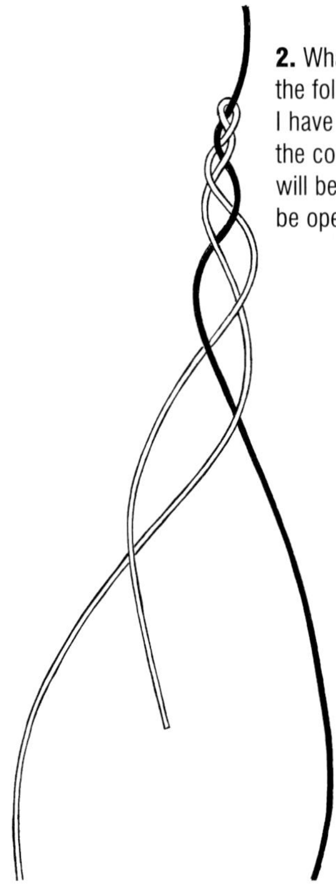

3. All that remains now is for you to finish of the Plait so that it can't come undone. In this case I've finished off the splice with a series of half hitches.

Plaiting a Double

1. With the source line doubled, the Plait is commenced by wrapping the returning tag around the main line or standing part to define the length of the doubled section.

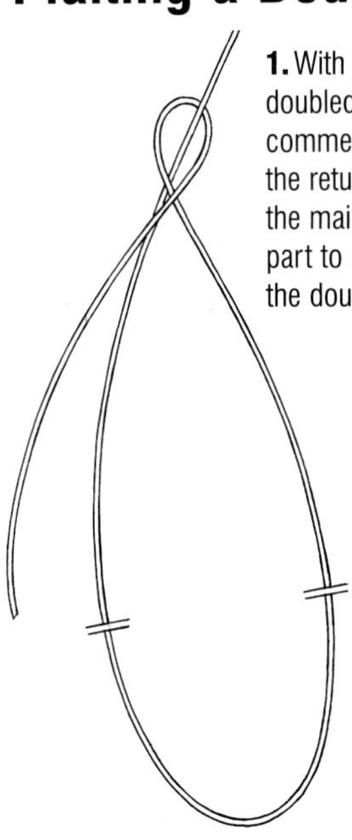

2. Maintaining tension on the main line, the plait is performed by passing the strand on each side alternately to the centre as we did in the first example of Plaiting.

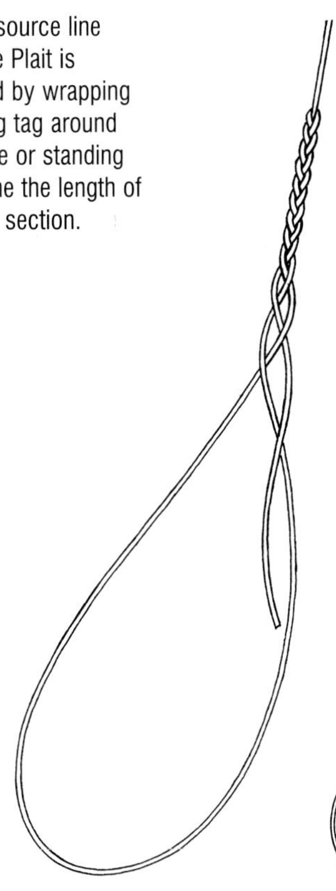

3. Having plaited an inch for every 10 lbs (4.5 kg) breaking strain of the line you can finish off by half hitching the tag several times around the other two strands.

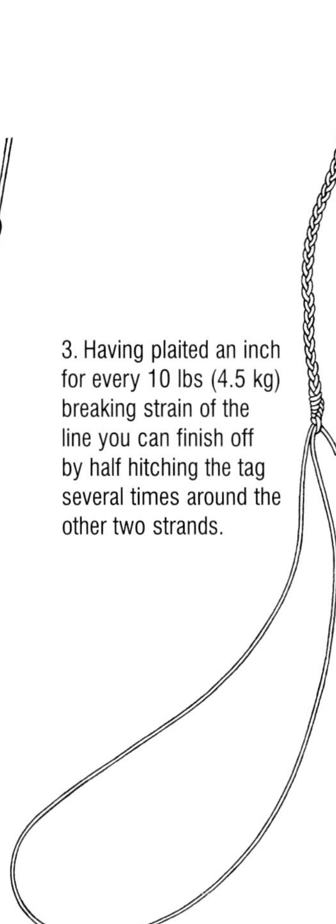

Summary

It would seem from the tests on the opposite page, and others I have done over the past sixteen years or so that I have had gelspun lines to test, that some suppliers of gelspun drastically understate the breaking strains of their lines; I guess to avoid conflict with good old boys who see no reason to learn new knots for new-fangled skinny lines.

On the other hand, learning to make sound connections that retain the additional strength possessed by at least some of these lines, puts a powerful tool for subduing large and powerful fish, in the hands of anglers seriously targeting large and powerful fish.

Some tests

I purchased two spools of gelspun line from a local fishing tackle store for the tests I performed for this chapter. One was a fused line and labelled “Berkley Fireline” the other was a braided line labelled “New Spiderwire Stealth Camo Braid”. Both were marked 10 lb and the diameter given for both was 0.008 inches (0.2 mm).

The first knots I tested were the Double Uni Knot and the Albright, both commonly used by gelspun aficionados for joining lines and attaching leaders.

Albright Knot

Tied to a nylon monofilament leader labelled “Stren High Impact Monofilament” 20 lb test and diameter 0.0177 inches (0.45 mm), the Albright, when tied in the Spiderwire sample broke at 8.6 lb (3.9 kg) or 86% of the stated breaking strain.

Tested in 10 lb Berkley Fireline the Albright also failed at 8.6 lb (3.9 kg) or 86% of the line’s stated breaking strain. Completely satisfactory results for a 10 lb (4.5 kg) breaking strain line.

Double Uni Knot

Two lengths of each line were each tied together with a Double Uni Knot using seven turns on each side. The Spiderwire failed at 11.7 lb (5.3 kg) or 117% of its stated breaking strain.

Tied in Berkley Fireline, the Double Uni Knot failed at 8.6 lb (3.9 kg) or 86% of the state breaking strain.

So once again, for a 10 lb breaking strain line that is a great result, but as further test showed, neither of these lines are 10 lb breaking strain.

Bimini Twist Double

First tying, then testing, a 50 turn Bimini Twist Double in both samples the Bimini remained intact as the line failed on the metal tube around which the line was wrapped in both cases. The Spiderwire failed at 19.4 lb (8.8 kg) or 194% of the stated breaking strain and the Berkley Fireline failed at 21.3 lb (9.7 kg) or 213% of the stated breaking strain. Remember, both of these lines were marked as 10 lb.

Bimini Cat’s Paw Splice

I wound up the Biminis on each side of the Cat’s Paw Splice so that only the splice was tested, first on the Spiderwire which collapsed the metal tube at just over 26.4 lb (12 kg) without breaking. Using a plastic tube I tested the Berkley Fireline to the same extent without it breaking, once again re-affirming the strength of this join.

Attaching Leader with a Bimini Plaited Splice

First tying a Bimini Double. Then plaiting that double with the 20 leader material in both lines, the following results were achieved.

The Spiderwire broke above the Bimini at 19.4 lb (8.8 kg) or 194% of the stated breaking strain. While the Fireline similarly broke on the plastic tube at 20.7 lb (9.4 kg) or 207% of the line’s stated breaking strain, again re-affirming the strength of this join.

Attaching a monofilament leader with a Plaited Splice

It’s possible to plait either a nylon or fluorocarbon monofilament leader using a single strand of gelspun line as I have illustrated, and it produces a sound connection. My concerns are with folk who promote this connection on You Tube and the like, under different names, as a 100% join. It is not. I tied it in both the test lines and got the following results.

Attaching a leader of the 20 lb Stren monofilament that I mentioned earlier to the 10 lb Spiderwire, the Plaited Splice broke at 15.6 lb (7.1 kg) or 156% of the Spiderwire’s stated breaking strain. Doing the same with the Fireline I got 11 lb (5.0 kg) or 110%. Repeating the test got almost the same result at 10.8 lb (4.9 kg) or 108%.

Joining two similar Gelspun Lines using a Plaited Splice

I’ve already mentioned a little rule that works very well when making a Plaited Double or Plaited Splice, either in monofilament or in gelspun, and that is to plait one inch (25 mm) for every 10 lb (4.5 kg) breaking strain the line tests at.

My first plaits in both of the tested gelspun lines were about one inch (25 mm), simply because they were both marked 10 lbs. And this would have remained perfectly fine had I not been testing these lines to destruction.

With disappointing results I extended the splices to just on 2 inches (50 mm) (which is correct for 20 lb (9.0 kg)) and got the following results:

Two lengths of the Spiderwire joined with a two inch Plaited Splice (no double) then tested, failed at 17.6 lb (8.0 kg), 176% while the same join in the Fireline failed at 17.4 lb (7.9 kg), 174%.

Chapter 8

LEADERS

An Introduction to Leaders

The terms leader and trace are sometimes confused, but for the purposes of this exercise, leaders refer to a length of heavier line that is attached to the main line coming from the reel, whereas the trace is a shorter length of fishing line, or wire, to which the hook or lure is attached.

Shock Leaders

Shock leaders are mainly used when it is necessary to introduce a length of heavier line to prevent break offs when casting. However, they may be attached to resist abrasion from rough ground, or when playing rough skinned fish like sharks.

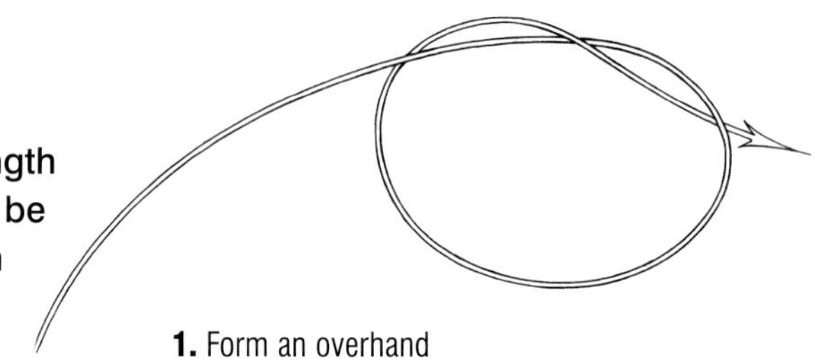

1. Form an overhand knot in the end of your leader.

Unfortunately, repetitive casts – as would be required for a lure casting session, sooner or later – destroy the leader knot through impact against the rod guides, particularly the stripping guide or first guide above the reel.

However, by extending the leader to three and a half or four rod lengths, that problem is greatly reduced.

Should fishing with a leader of this length be problematic, the alternative, in my experience anyway, is to keep the leader short enough so that it cannot be wound in through the rod guides and onto the reel.

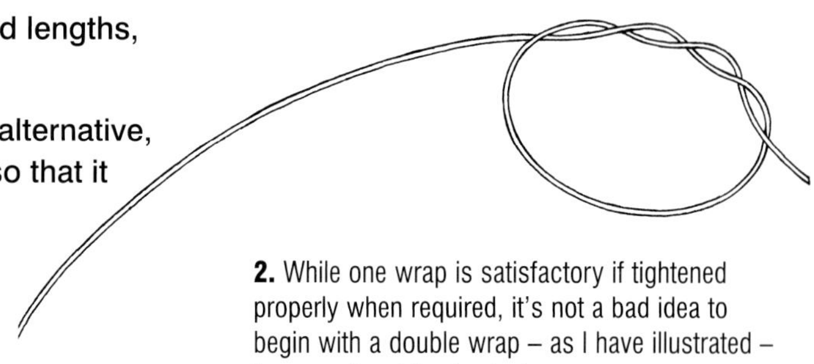

2. While one wrap is satisfactory if tightened properly when required, it's not a bad idea to begin with a double wrap – as I have illustrated – for security, at the beginning anyway.

Shock Leader Knot

Of the various shock leader knots I have used, I have found this one the most satisfactory. It works best when the line being used as a shock leader is about twice the breaking strain of the main line coming from the reel and when both line and leader are nylon monofilament.

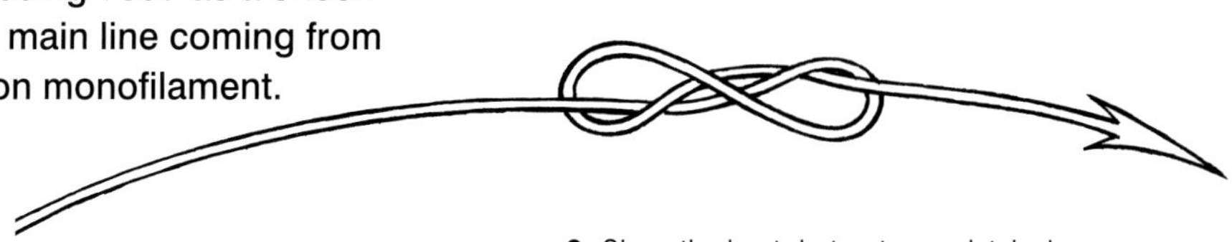

3. Close the knot, but not completely, because you'll have to thread the lighter line through it.

Materials required

You will require a slim metal tube to tie this knot. I use 1/16 inch OD, 1/32 inch ID brass tubes manufactured by K&S Engineering , Chicago, USA. I've also used a Lumbar Puncture needle. The brass tubing is available in 12 inch (30 cm) lengths from the model aircraft departments of leading hobby shops. You may obtain a Lumbar Puncture from a medical equipment supplier. Most commercially produced nail knotting tools, the ones to come my way at least, are too coarse for use with the relatively light lines used for beach and inshore fishing.

Naturally, you will need line and leader: In the preparation of these drawings, I used for a main line, a spool of monofilament marked Platypus Classic 15 lb with a diameter of 0.013 inch (0.35 mm). For a leader, I used a spool of monofilament marked Black Magic Line 40 lb with a diameter of 0.022 inch (0.56 mm) and found that to be a good combination.

Because the slim brass tubes that I use for making nail knots soon discolour and consequently are not easily located having put them aside after use, I slide an 0.33 inch (8 mm) coloured plastic bead over the tube and stick it in place. Doing this will enable you to re-locate the tube more easily.

4. I've shaded the lighter line here so you can see more clearly how it's threaded through the knot in the leader.

5. Close the knot in the leader a bit more, but not so tightly that you cannot pull more of the leader through, then, introduce the slim metal tube.

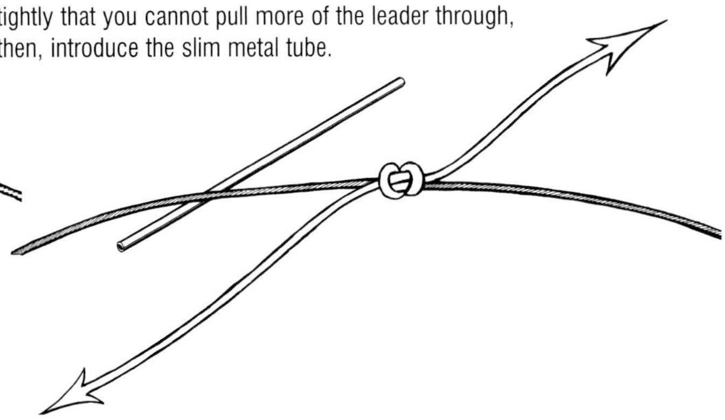

6. Lay the tube alongside the leader and begin wrapping the main line and leader as shown. The wraps should be tight. I've only opened them up so that you can see the process more clearly.

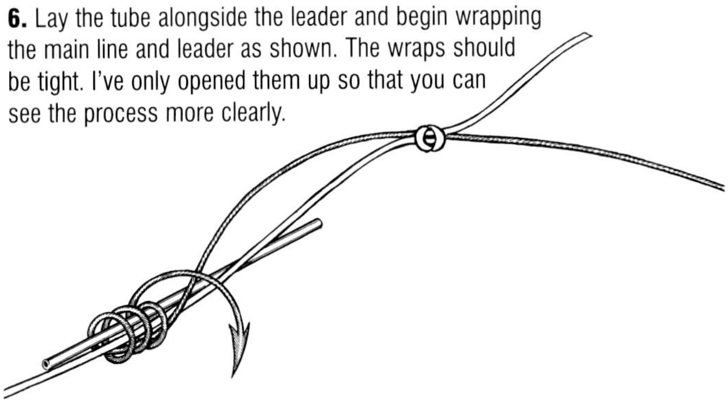

7. I suggest making a minimum of eight wraps, but not more than twelve, before threading the tube with the tag of the main line. Using more than twelve wraps, as I have on occasion, may result in a finished knot with some loose loops, something best avoided.

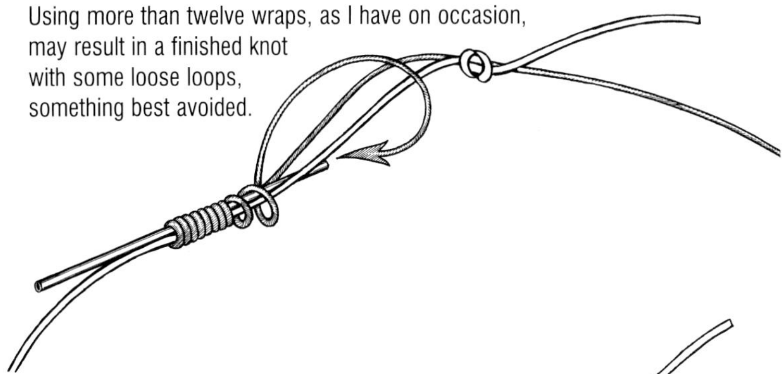

8. Withdraw the tube and with it the main line tag.

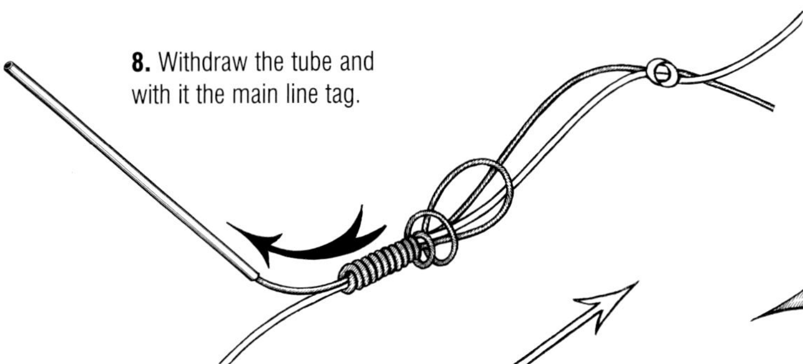

9. Tighten the nail knot in the main line.

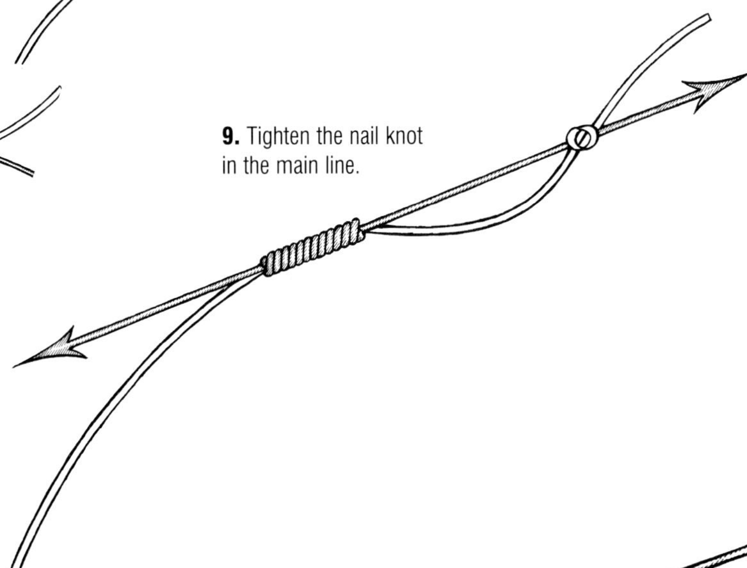

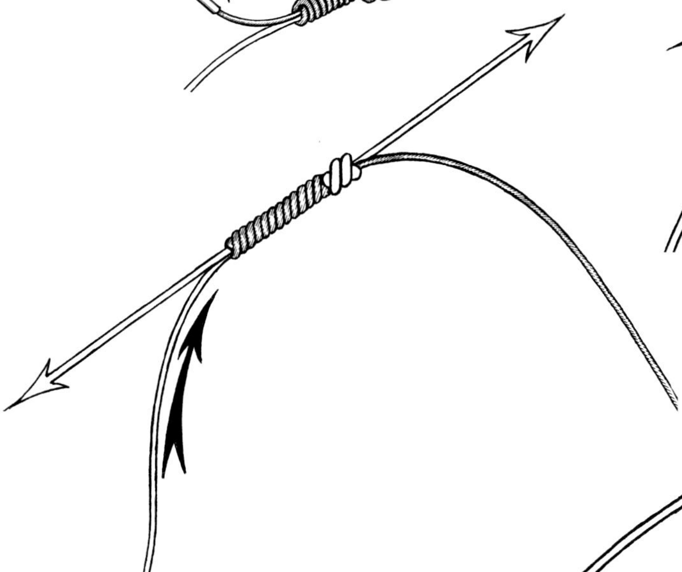

10. Slide the two knots together and tighten each in turn until the whole entity looks firm and streamlined.

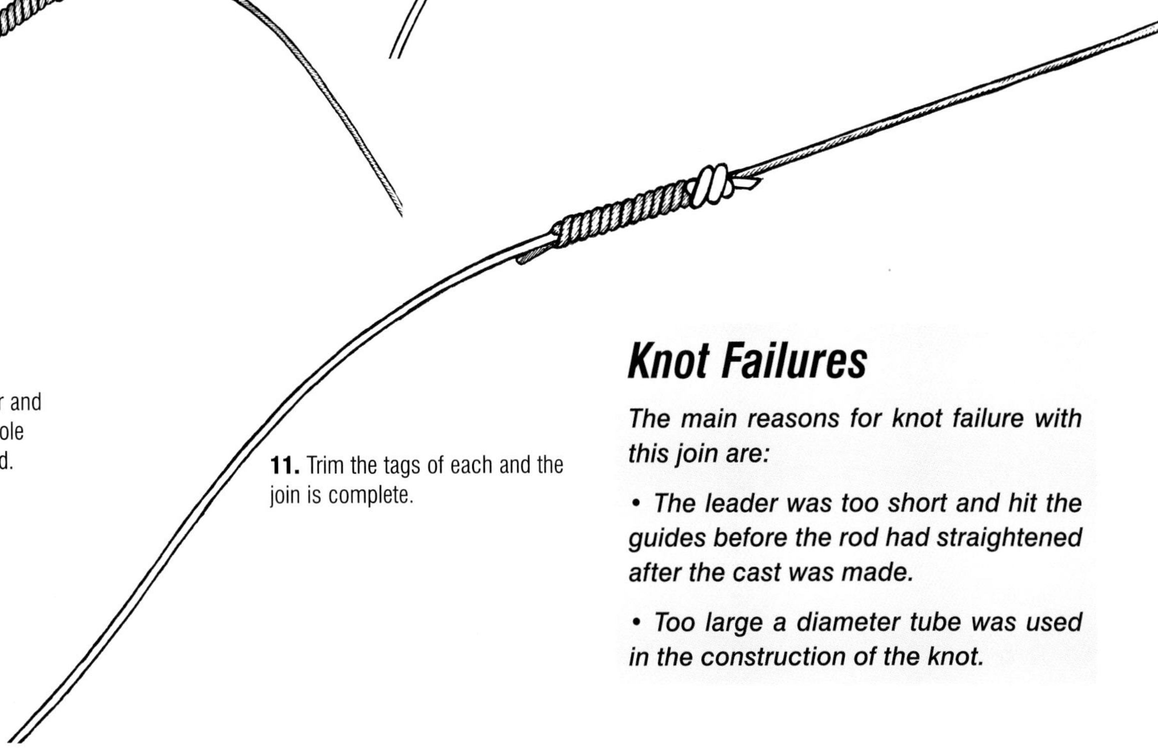

11. Trim the tags of each and the join is complete.

Knot Failures

The main reasons for knot failure with this join are:

- *The leader was too short and hit the guides before the rod had straightened after the cast was made.*
- *Too large a diameter tube was used in the construction of the knot.*

Tony Jones Leader Knot

This leader knot has several names including Deckies Leader Knot and Ducknose Leader Knot. In other publications I have referred to it as Tony Jones' Leader Knot, because charter boat skipper, Tony Jones, showed it to me.

When used in Gelspun line I have referred to it as a Braid Leader Knot (another of its names). However, it can be used both in gelspun and monofilament lines: The point to remember is that when joining a monofilament leader to a gelspun line more wraps have to be used.

Similarly, the closer the diameter of both lines, the more wraps that are required. The greater the difference in diameter between the two lines, the fewer the wraps that are required.

Knot Failures

This knot may fail, or not form properly, for the following reasons:

• The tag was released too soon, preventing the knot from forming.

• There may be insufficient wraps. For example; when attaching a relatively light monofilament leader to a light gelspun line, twenty or more wraps may be required.

• Conversely, if the leader is disproportionately heavy the knot mightn't close.

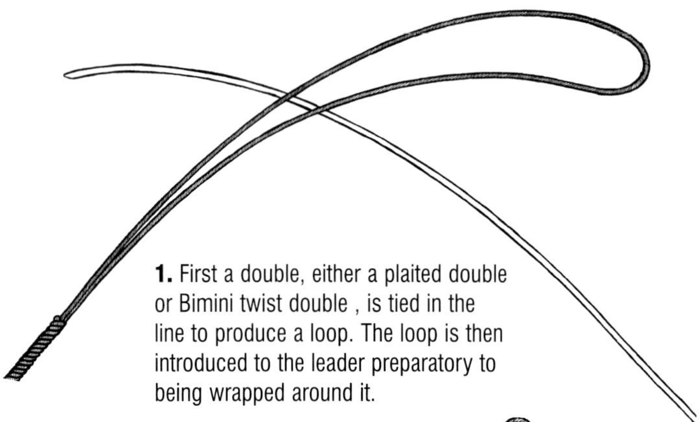

1. First a double, either a plaited double or Bimini twist double , is tied in the line to produce a loop. The loop is then introduced to the leader preparatory to being wrapped around it.

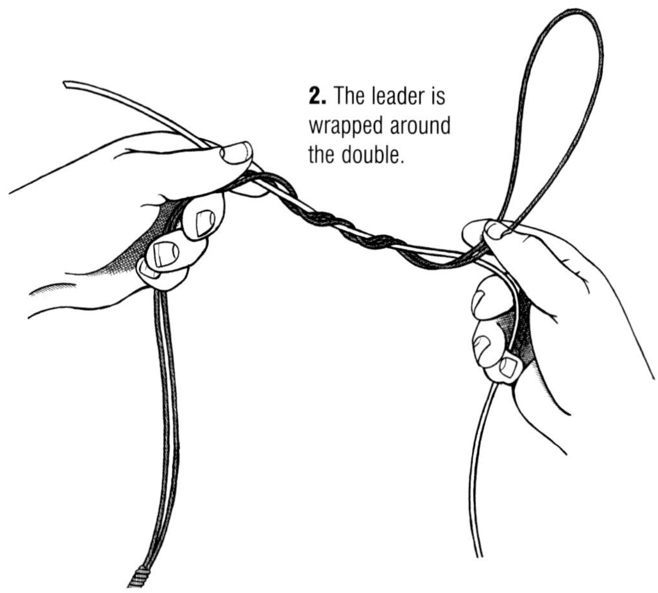

2. The leader is wrapped around the double.

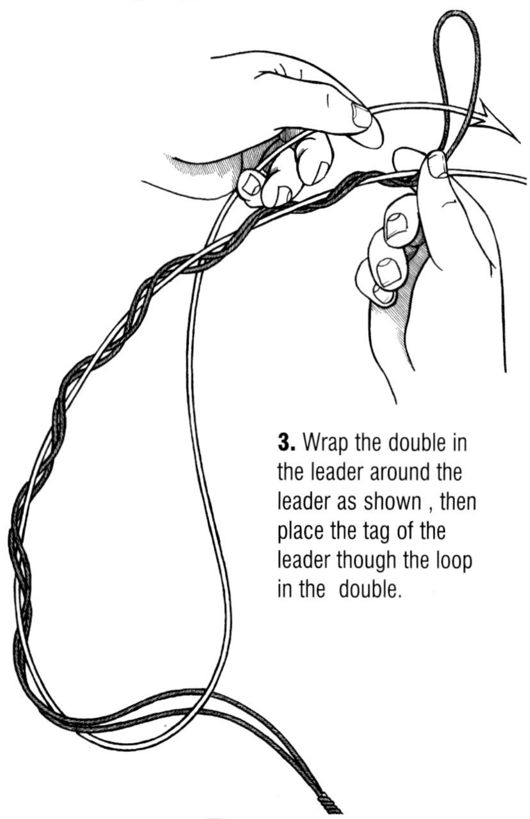

3. Wrap the double in the leader around the leader as shown , then place the tag of the leader though the loop in the double.

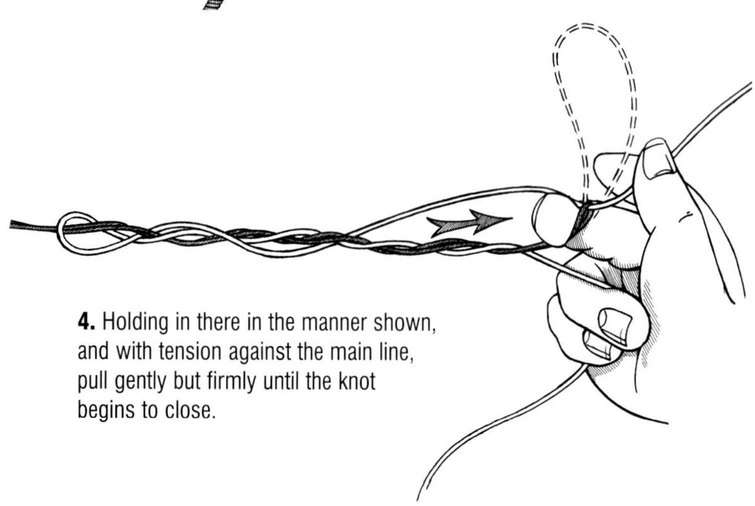

4. Holding in there in the manner shown, and with tension against the main line, pull gently but firmly until the knot begins to close.

5. As the double in the main line straightens, transferring those wraps to the leader, you can release the tag and tension the leader against the main line.

6. Having trimmed the leader tag, the knot is complete.

Wind-on Leaders

The leaders so far discussed can be wound in through the guides and onto the reel and therefore could be termed wind-on leaders. However, the term Wind-on Leader usually refers to monofilament leaders, usually nylon, but sometimes fluorocarbon, fitted with a loop-spliced dacron or gelspun or other hollow sleeve enabling their attachment to a Bimini or Plaited Double in the end of the main line.

They are mainly used when game fishing on the high seas over rods that have been fitted with roller guides, but they are sometimes used with ringed guides, and in other fishing applications as well.

Materials

The materials I used in this exercise were:

- 30 inches (75 cm) of 130 lb (60 kg) dacron.
- Some single strand stainless wire; diameter 0.02 inch (0.5 mm).
- 26 feet (8 m) of 0.07 inch (1.8 mm) bulk nylon monofilament.
- Scalpel.
- Nail Clippers
- 100 and 250 grit sandpaper.
- Some 30 lb (13.6 kg) braided gelspun line

Splicing Needle

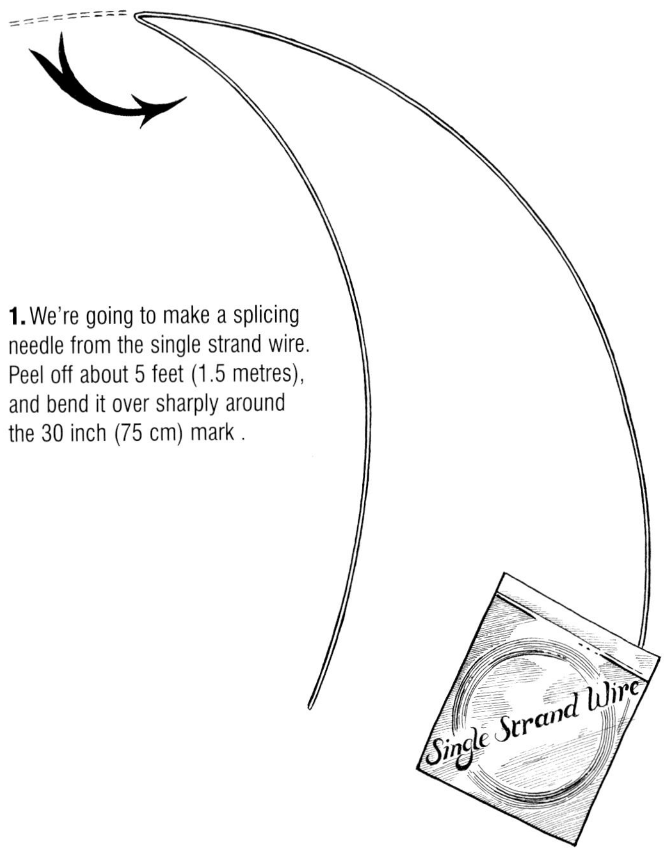

1. We're going to make a splicing needle from the single strand wire. Peel off about 5 feet (1.5 metres), and bend it over sharply around the 30 inch (75 cm) mark .

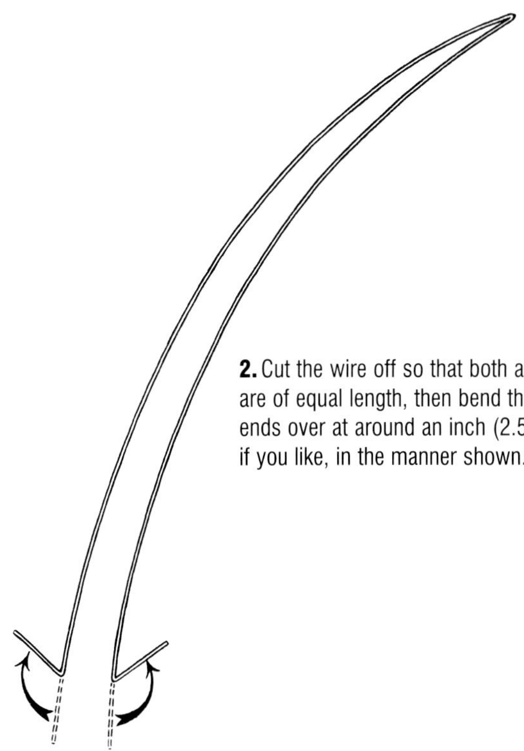

2. Cut the wire off so that both arms are of equal length, then bend the ends over at around an inch (2.5 cm) if you like, in the manner shown.

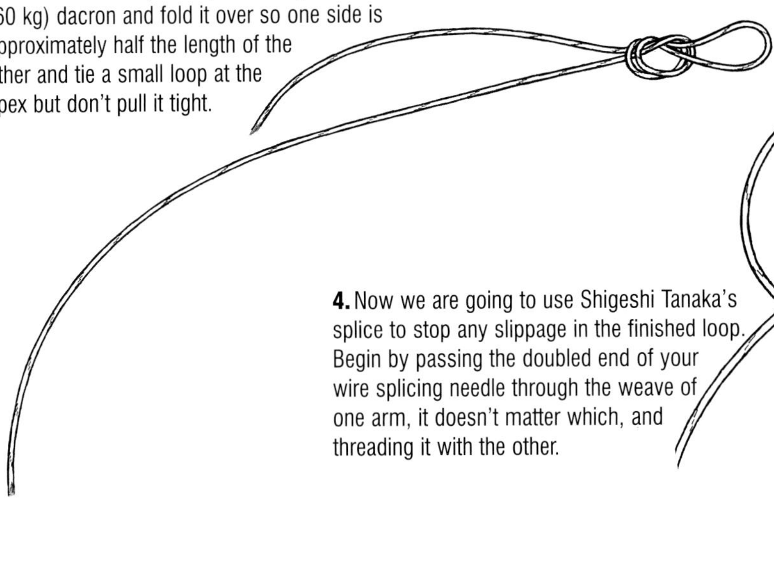

3. Take 30 inches (75 cm) or so of your 130 lb (60 kg) dacron and fold it over so one side is approximately half the length of the other and tie a small loop at the apex but don't pull it tight.

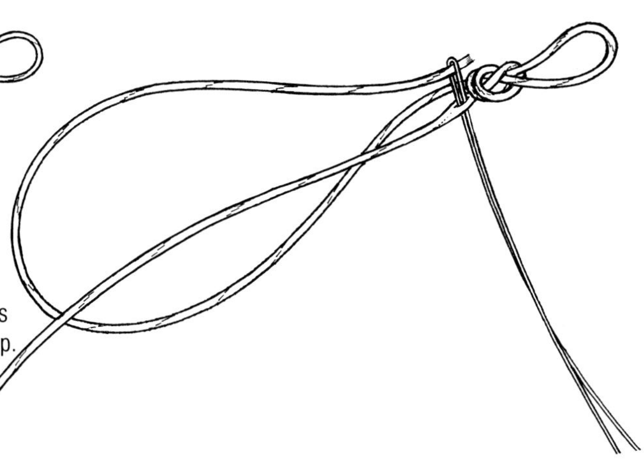

4. Now we are going to use Shigeshi Tanaka's splice to stop any slippage in the finished loop. Begin by passing the doubled end of your wire splicing needle through the weave of one arm, it doesn't matter which, and threading it with the other.

continued next page...

5. Then pulling it through.

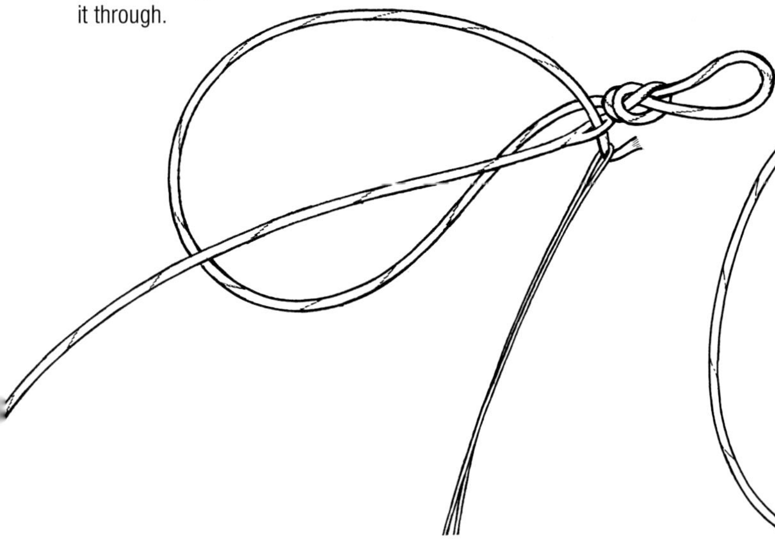

6. The process is repeated with the opposite number.

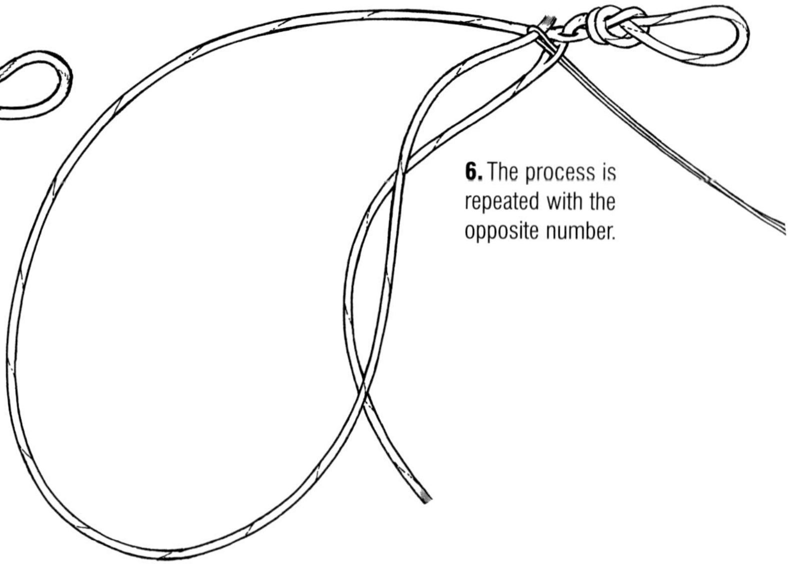

7. And so on.

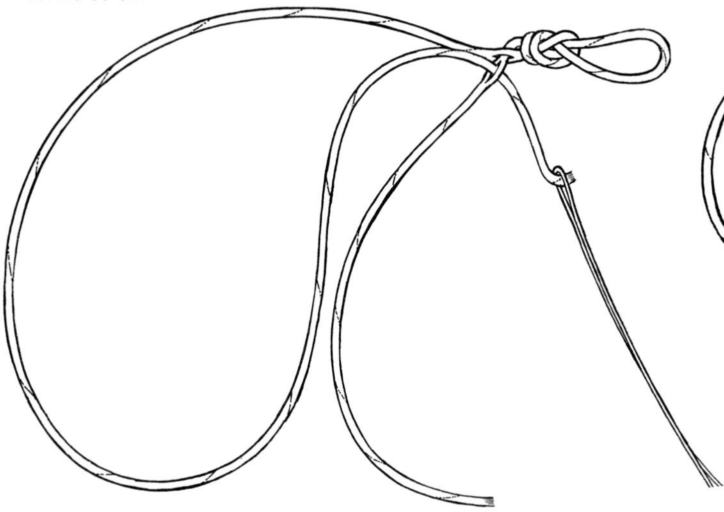

8. Until the effect shown is produced, finishing up with the shorter arm protruding.

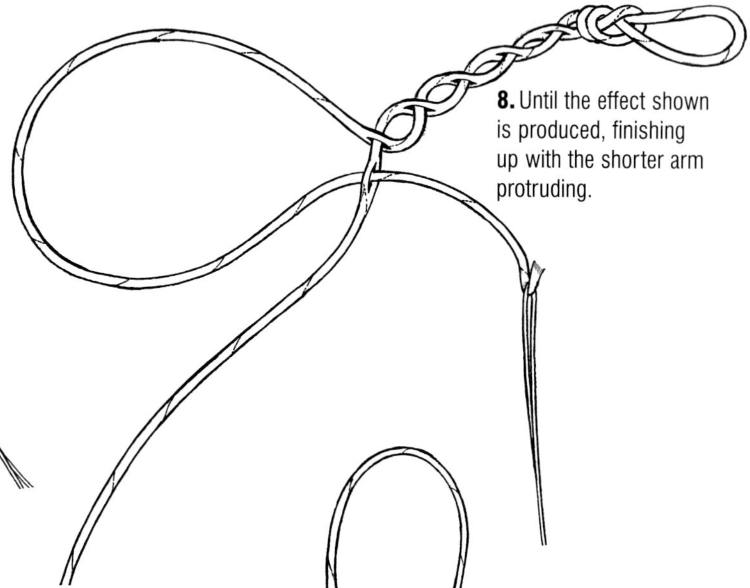

9. Undo the loop your first tied in the dacron.

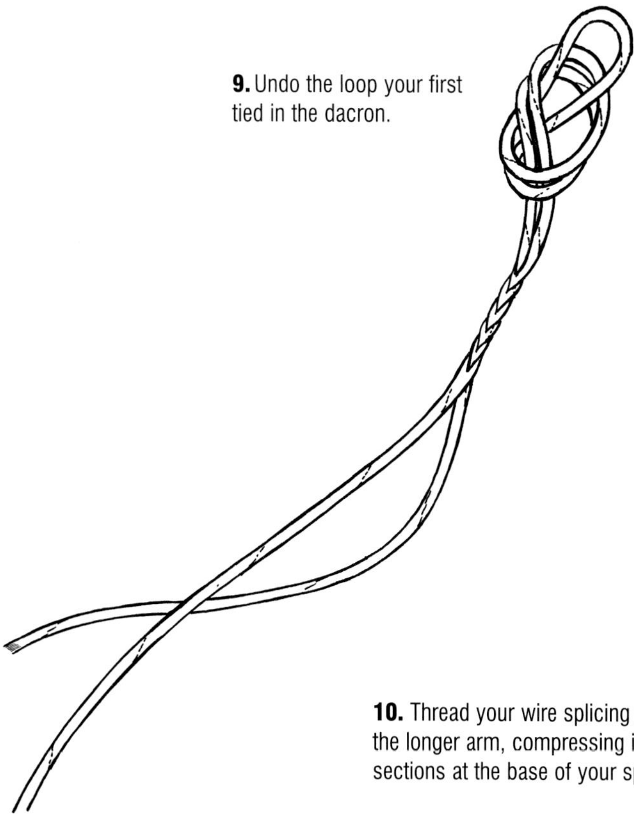

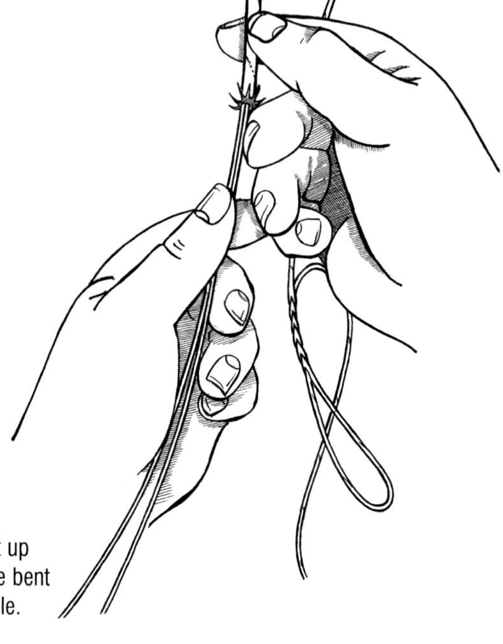

10. Thread your wire splicing needle right up the longer arm, compressing it against the bent sections at the base of your splicing needle.

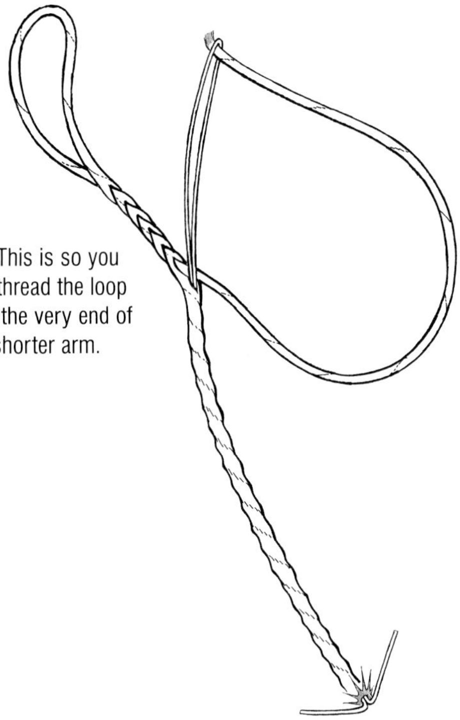

11. This is so you can thread the loop with the very end of the shorter arm.

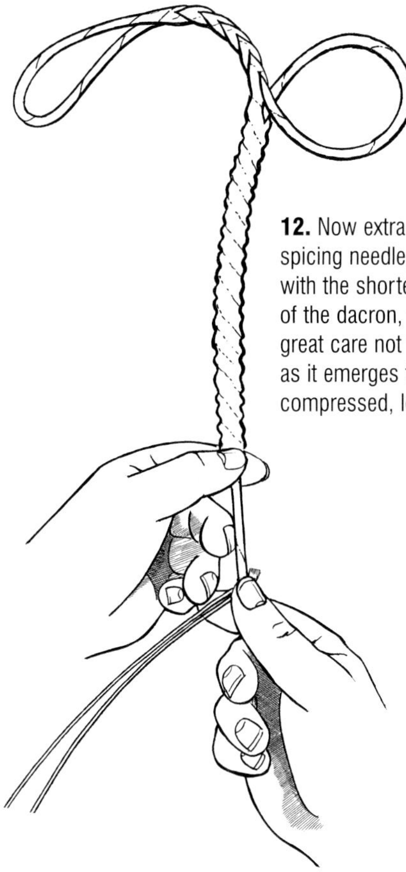

12. Now extract your spicing needle, along with the shorter arm of the dacron, taking great care not to lose it as it emerges from the compressed, longer arm.

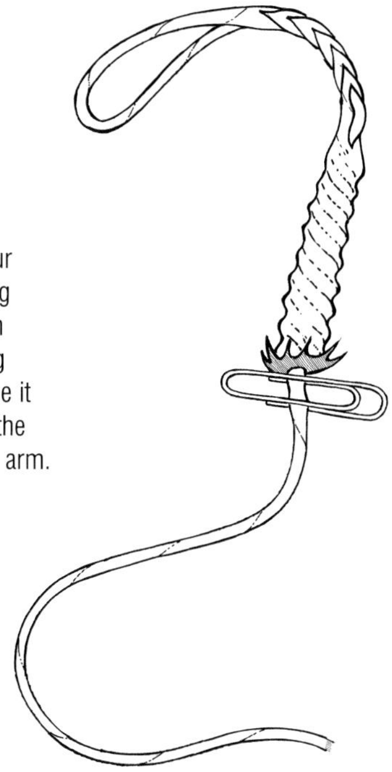

13. Pull the shorter arm out as far as it will go, compressing the longer arm tightly, and use a large paper clip or the like to hold it in place.

14. Take your scalpel and taper the end of the monofilament leader down, but not so much that it makes a sharp point that will spear through the weave.

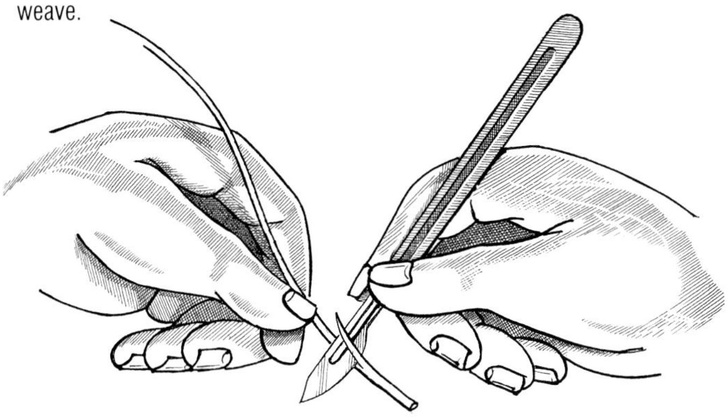

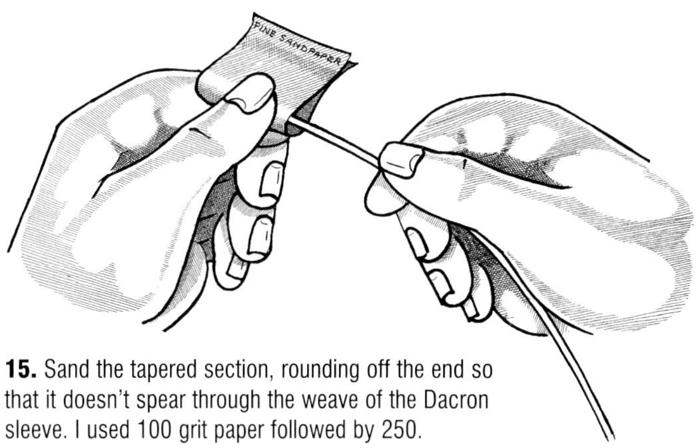

15. Sand the tapered section, rounding off the end so that it doesn't spear through the weave of the Dacron sleeve. I used 100 grit paper followed by 250.

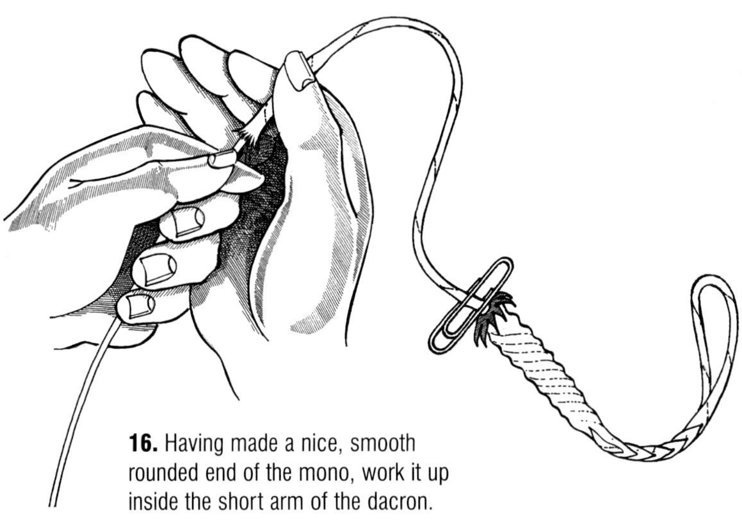

16. Having made a nice, smooth rounded end of the mono, work it up inside the short arm of the dacron.

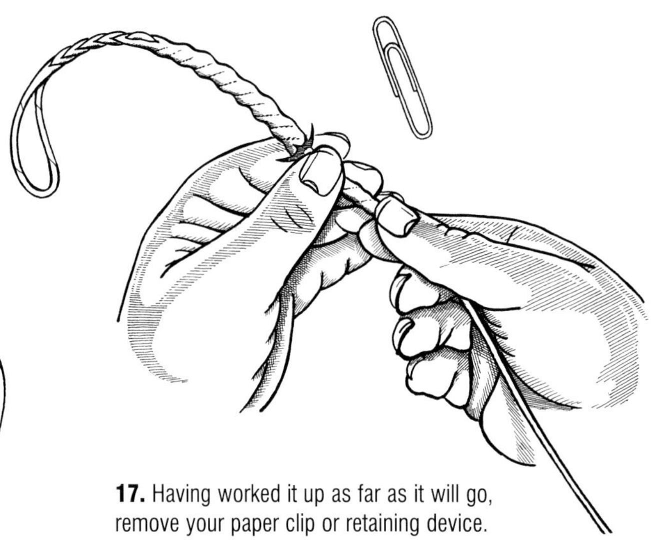

17. Having worked it up as far as it will go, remove your paper clip or retaining device.

continued next page...

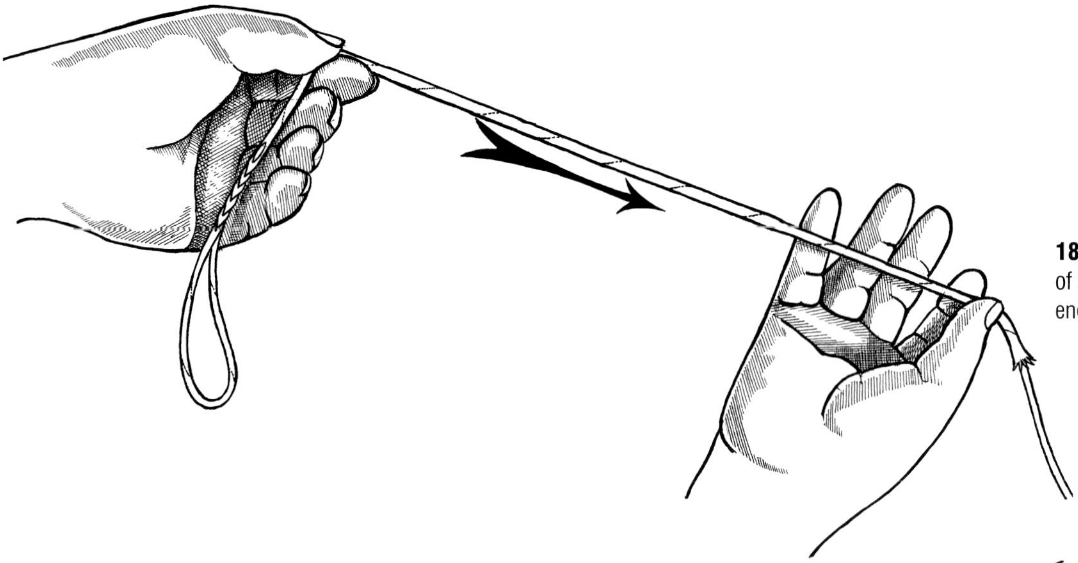

18. Then, gently work the longer arm of the Dacron back over the shorter end until it is fully extended.

19. Using your nail clippers, remove the frayed end of the dacron sleeve.

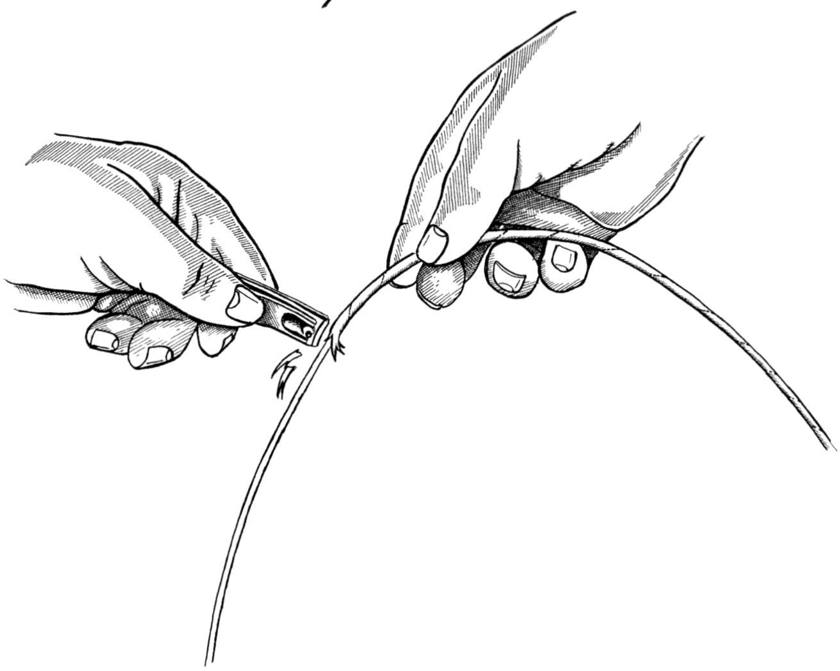

20. Take your gelspun line and cut off 3 feet (a metre) to facilitate the bound finish. You will also need to tie a small loop from the gelspun line to use as a pull through to finish off the binding.

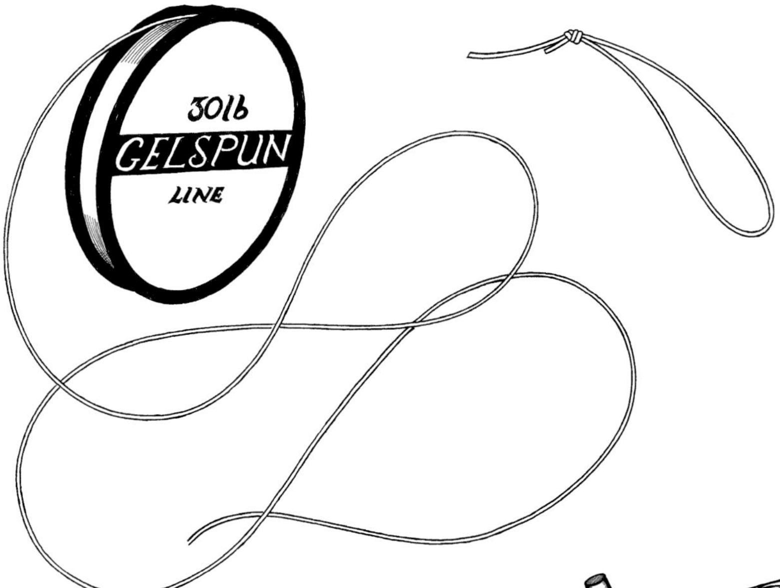

21. At this point the leader needs to be stretched tight between two fixed points and a binding with the gelspun line made to prevent the dacron being pushed off the monofilament leader. The binding is anchored on the mono leader just below the dacron sleeve using a clove hitch to which I have added some extra wraps. You may also want to tie a single overhand knot in the gelspun tag so you can pull it up really tight on the mono without the risk of it slipping undone.

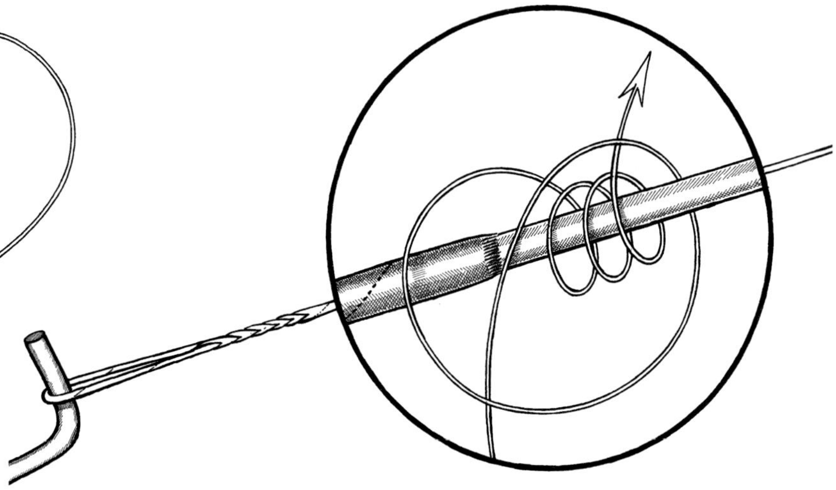

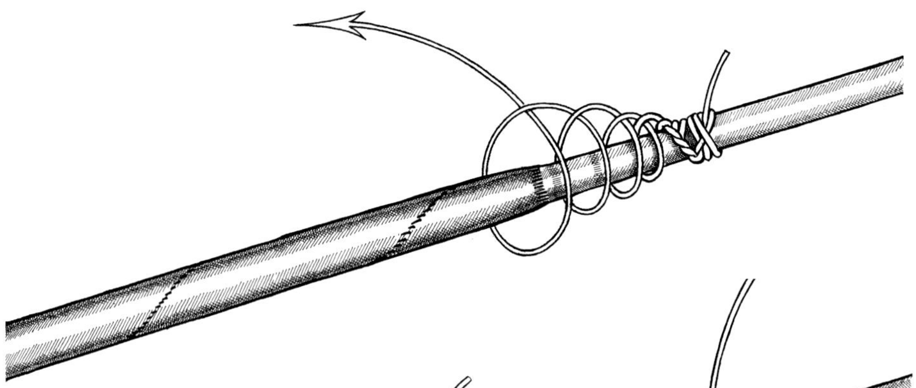

22. Now make a series of half hitches, pulling them firmly up against the anchor knot on the monofilament leader, but I have shown them open at this stage so you can see what is going on.

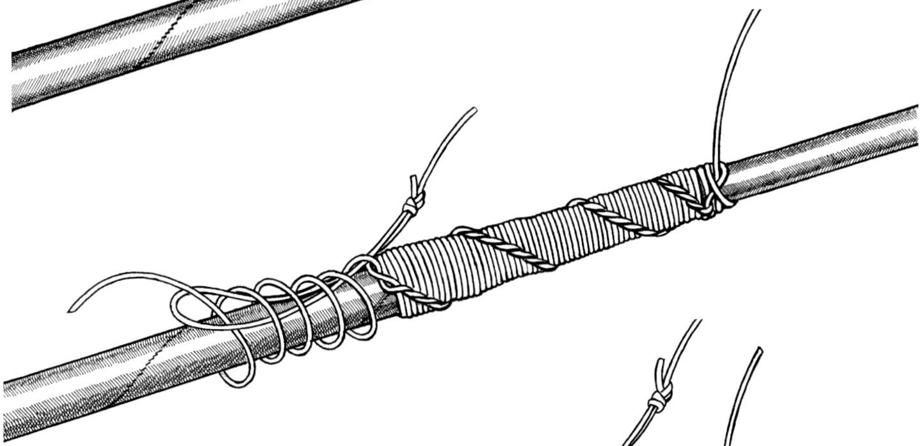

23. Having continued your series of half hitches up and over the end of the dacron, inset the loop of gelspun line and overbind it with ten or so wraps.

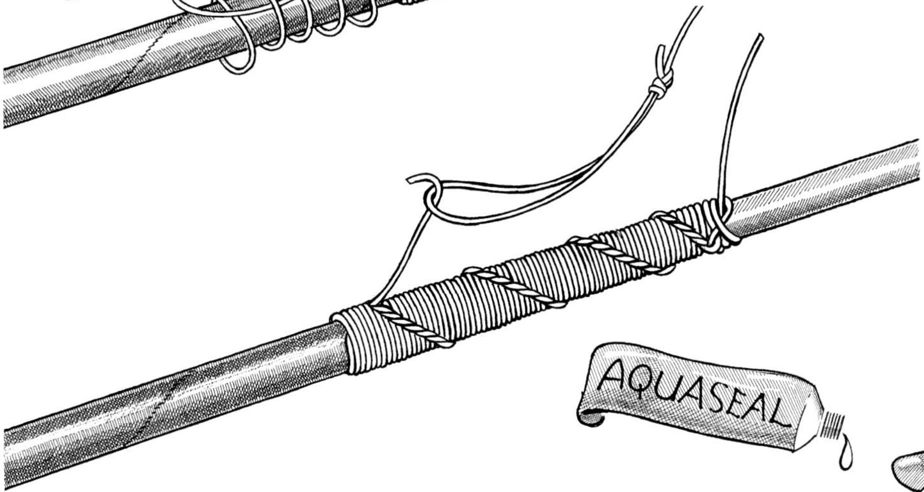

24. Extract the loop and tighten the binding by pulling gently but firmly on the tag.

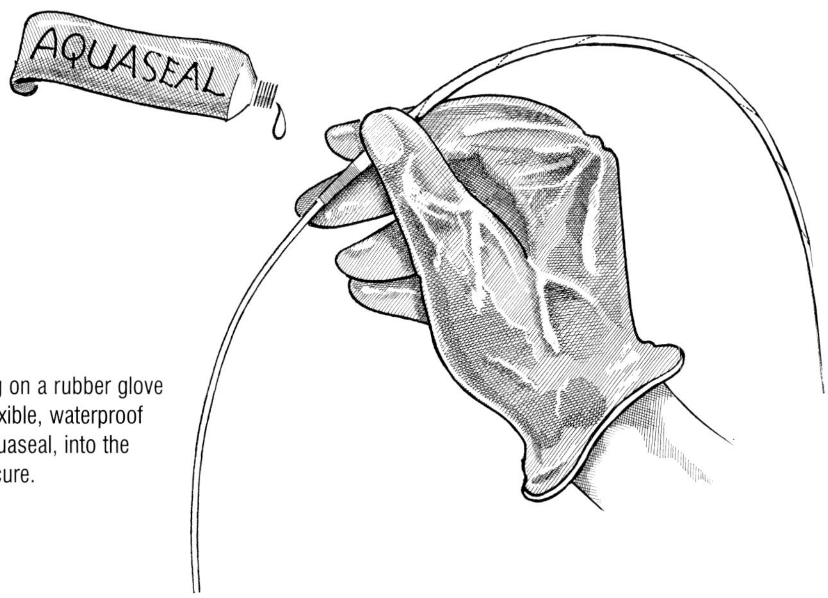

25. Finish off by putting on a rubber glove and massaging your flexible, waterproof sealant, in this case Aquaseal, into the binding and allow it to cure.

In Conclusion

Bear in mind this is an introduction to Wind-on Leaders for which I used two different sets of materials as the basis for this illustrative exercise: 130 lb (60 kg) IGFA dacron and 800 lb (360 kg) Jerry Brown's Hollow Spectra for the leader splices and two different materials:
0.071 inch (1.8 mm) diameter monofilament (stated test 450 lb or 200 kg) for the former and 0.118 inch (3 mm) diameter monofilament (stated test 900 lb or 400 kg) for the latter.

Although the process for each set of materials was the same, I noticed the Spectra had a looser weave and snagged more easily than the Dacron. For this reason, the mono leader end needed to be very smooth. The second was that if I didn't make the splice long enough – when some really serious pressure was applied – the monofilament leader could be pulled out, in some cases partially cooking the Spectra sleeve with the heat generated by the friction involved.

This problem was overcome by beginning with a longer sleeve: I finished up using 6 feet (1.8 metre) of the Spectra and lightly sanding the monofilament leader with a fine grit, the – section to go inside the sleeve – to give it a better grip. Doing that, I couldn't pull it out, not even with my Toyota and the gate post. The components would break but the splice remained intact.

Attaching Wind-on Leaders using the Cat's Paw

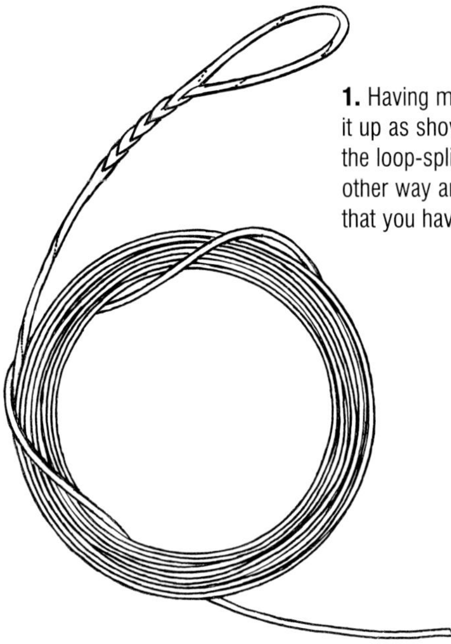

1. Having made your wind-on leader, coil it up as shown, beginning at the end with the loop-spliced sleeve. If you do it the other way around you will soon discover that you have a problem.

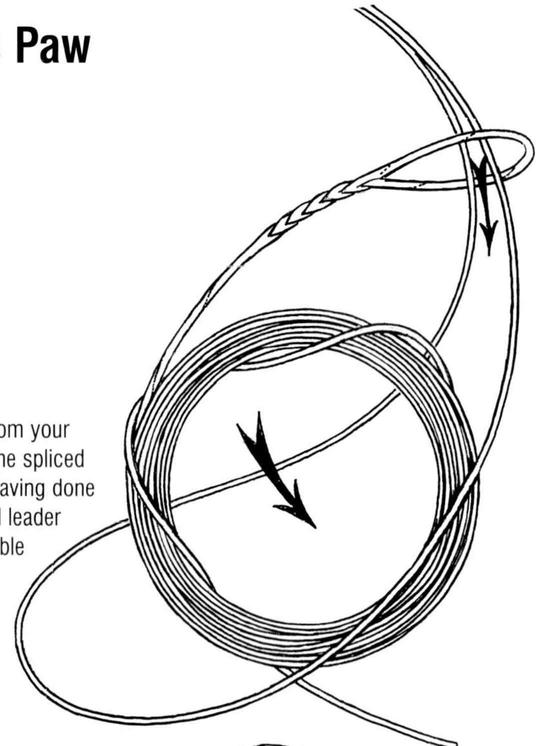

2. Pass the double from your rod and reel though the spliced loop in your leader. Having done that, pass your coiled leader back through the double in your line.

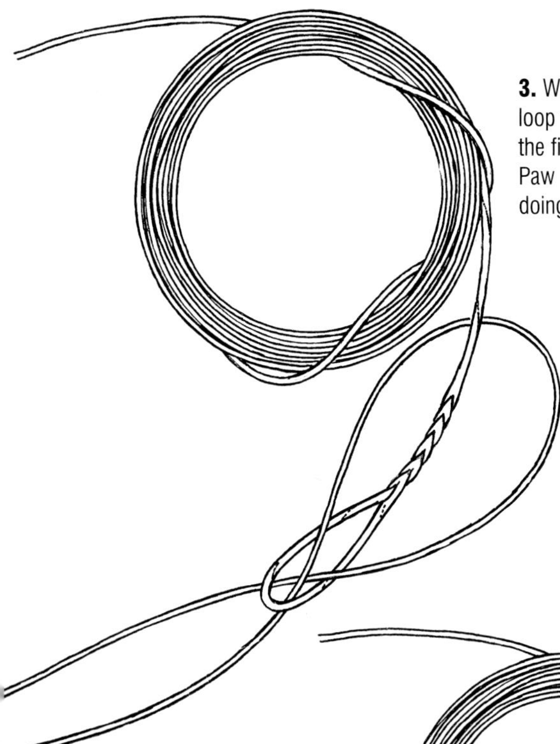

3. What you have now is a simple loop to loop connection, which is the first step in forming the Cat's Paw connection favoured by most doing this exercise.

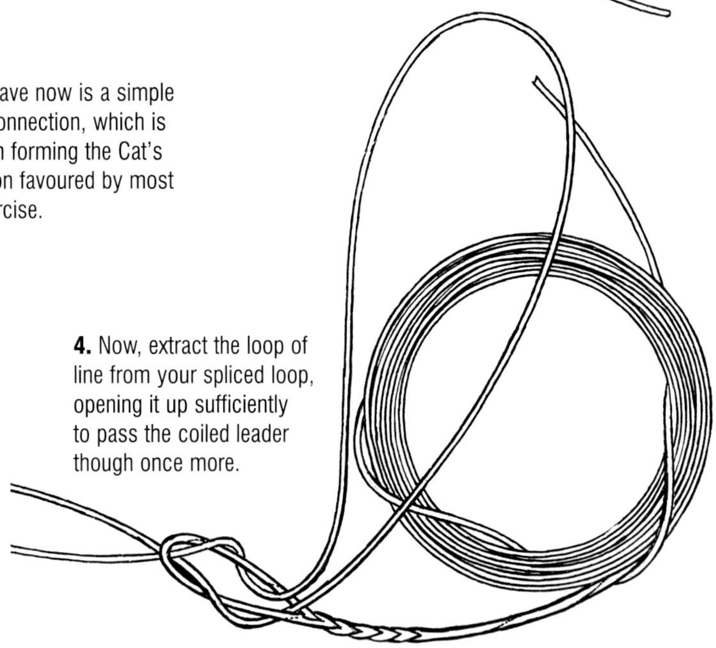

4. Now, extract the loop of line from your spliced loop, opening it up sufficiently to pass the coiled leader though once more.

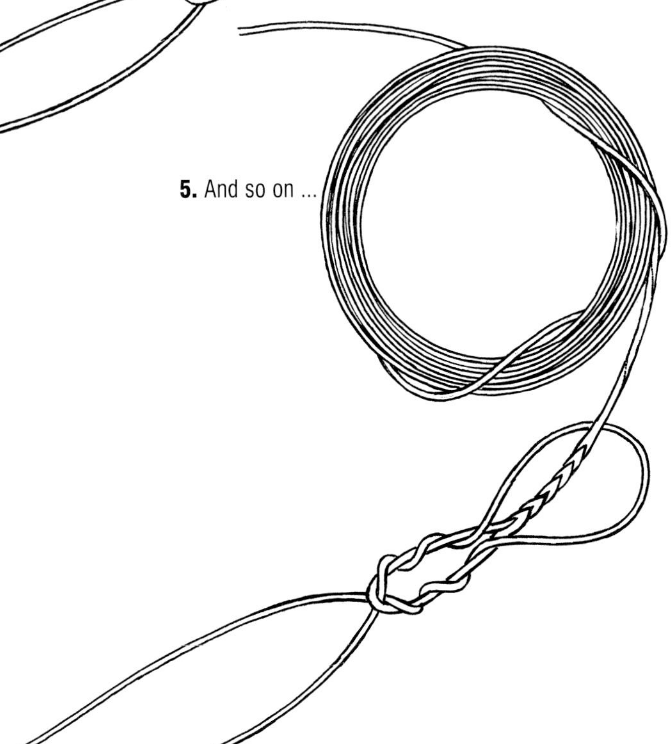

5. And so on ...

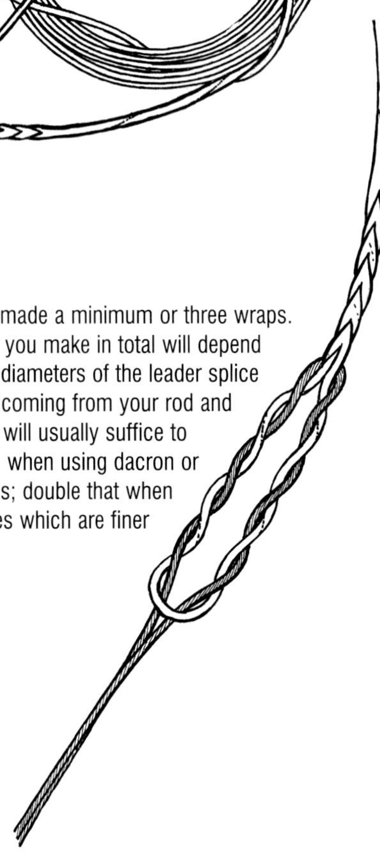

6. Until you have made a minimum or three wraps. How many wraps you make in total will depend on the respective diameters of the leader splice and the main line coming from your rod and reel. Three wraps will usually suffice to distribute the load when using dacron or monofilament lines; double that when using gelspun lines which are finer for a given test.

Attaching a Snap Swivel using the Nail Knot with a Loop

Attaching a heavy-duty snap-swivel to your leader enables the easy attachment of fairly short (about 6 feet (1.8 metre)) traces. Of course you could just select a metal sleeve of the appropriate size making a loop to hold the swivel and finish off by crimping the metal sleeve onto the loop in the leader, but you wouldn't need a knot book for that.

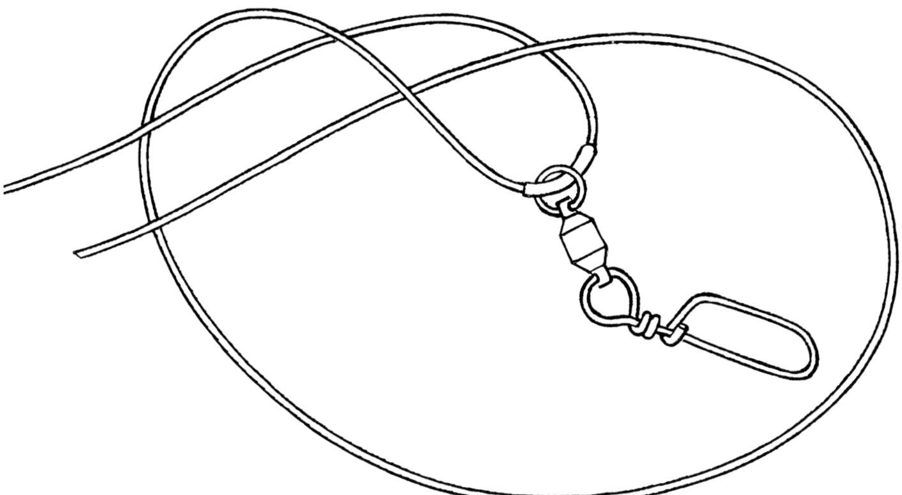

1. Thread the ring of the swivel and make the double loop configuration shown. You may add a short length of heavy duty plastic sleeve or armour spring of the appropriate diameter to give some protection from abrasion by the swivel.

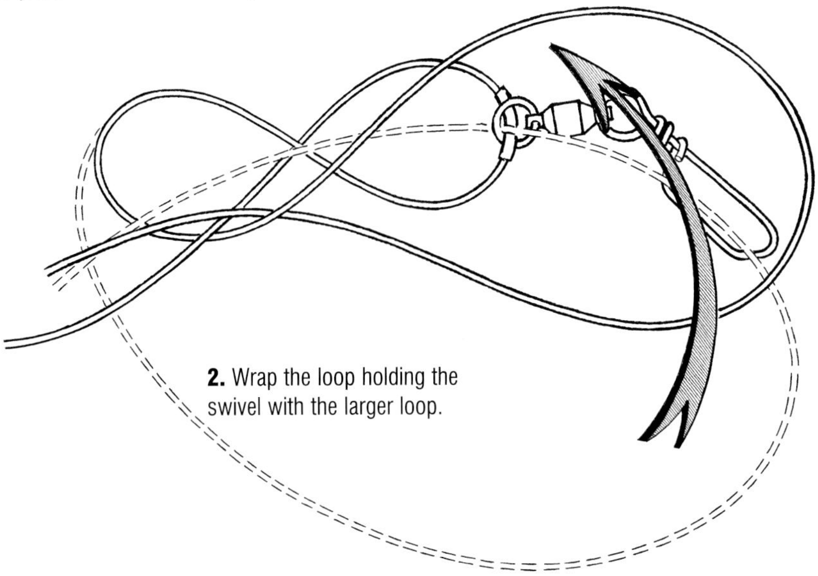

2. Wrap the loop holding the swivel with the larger loop.

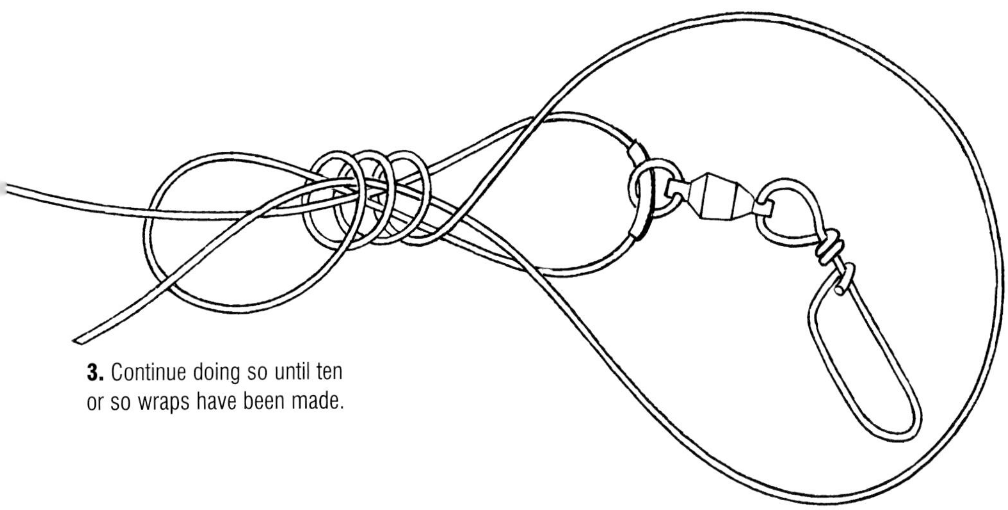

3. Continue doing so until ten or so wraps have been made.

4. Attach the swivel to a fixed object and tension the knot, initially by pulling on the main line. Then, when the knot has settled – and while still applying pressure to the main line – close the knot by tensioning the tag.

Chapter 9

TRACES

Traces: Some examples

Having constructed a wind-on leader with a swivel on the end for the attachment of traces in the previous chapter, it's time to look a couple of examples of widely used traces.

Making a Cable Trace

Wire cable, either with seven or forty nine strands, is used to catch sharks and other fish with teeth that would bite through a nylon or flurocarbon monofilament leader.

You will need a length of cable or multistrand wire that is compatible with the tackle you are using, and with I.G.F.A. line class tackle that will be about five times the breaking strain of your line.

For example with 30 lb (15 kg) tackle, choose cable of 150 lb (70 kg) test. Use 250 lb (110 kg) cable for 50 lb (24 kg), 400 lb (180 kg) for 80 lb (37 kg) and so on. It's a useful guide that helps avoid mismatched tackle but it is by no means the last word. There is room for flexibility.

I suggest beginning with two metres of cable, sleeves or swages of the correct size, and a crimping tool to attach those swages to the wire. You will also need a suitable hook like the Mustad 7699.

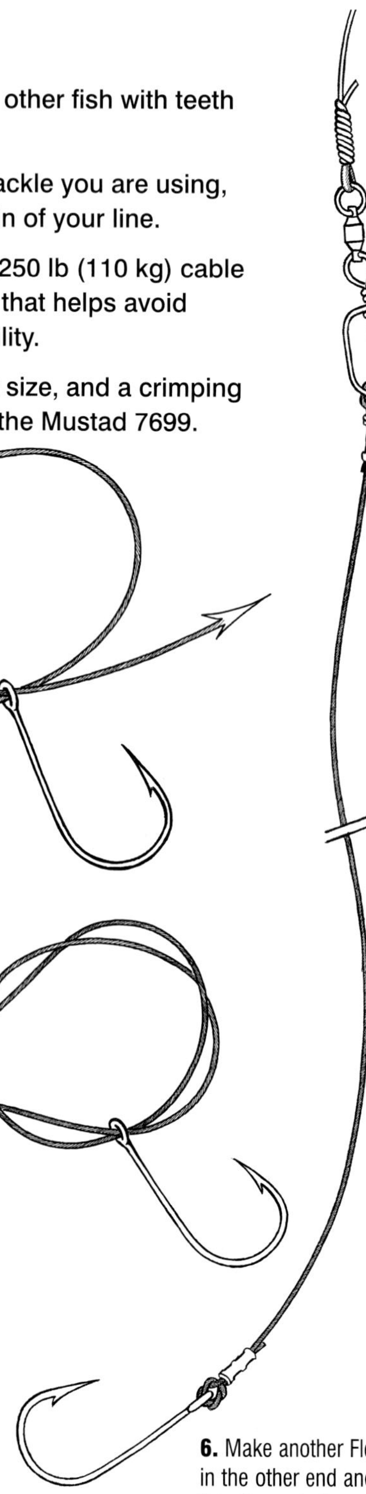

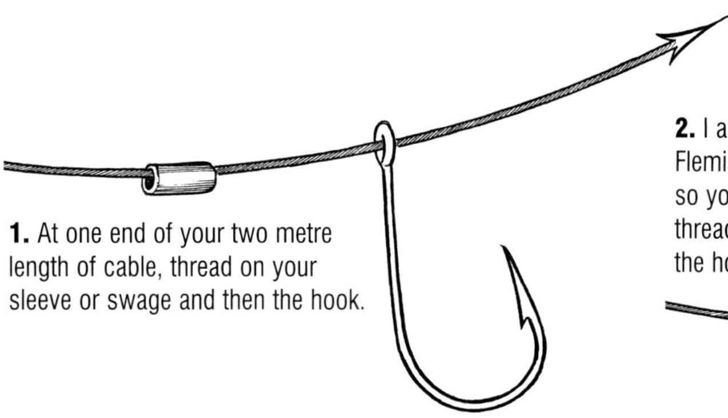

1. At one end of your two metre length of cable, thread on your sleeve or swage and then the hook.

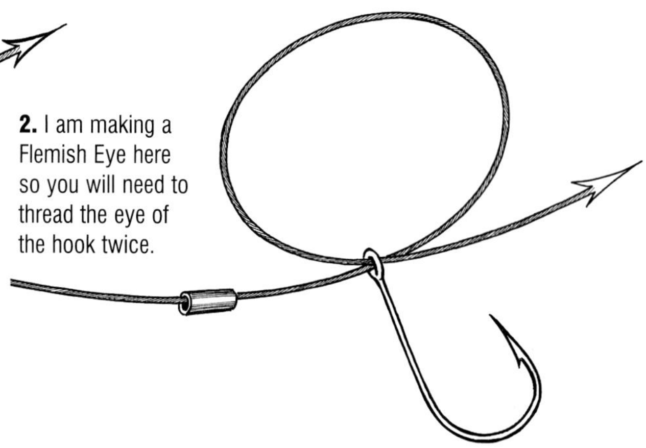

2. I am making a Flemish Eye here so you will need to thread the eye of the hook twice.

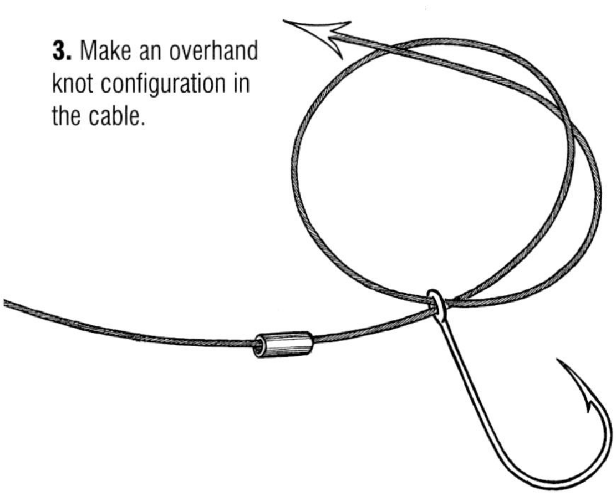

3. Make an overhand knot configuration in the cable.

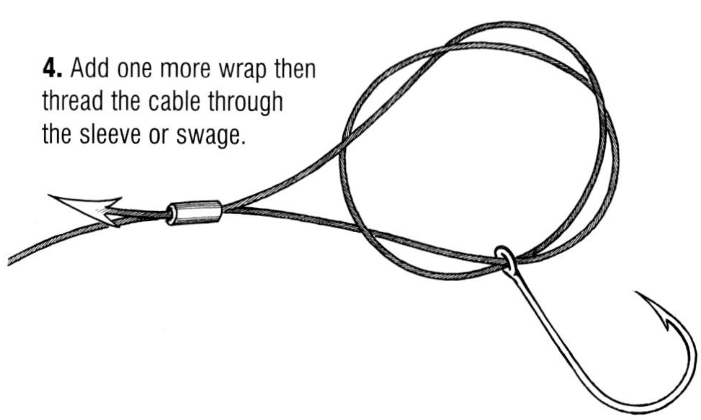

4. Add one more wrap then thread the cable through the sleeve or swage.

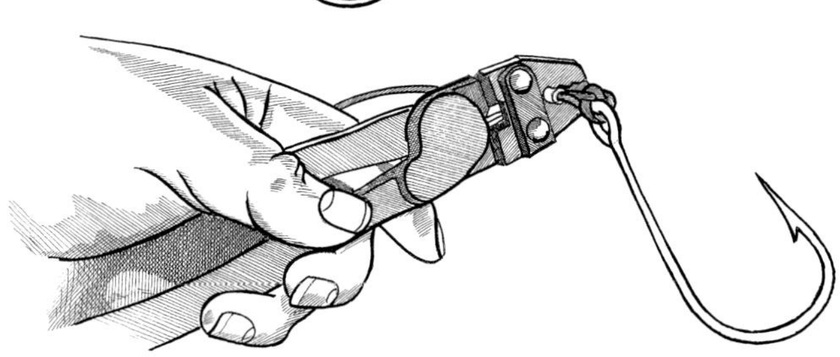

5. Close up the Flemish Eye and crimp the swage firmly in position.

6. Make another Flemish eye in the other end and connect it to the swivel on you wind-on leader as shown.

Making a Lure Trace

Skirted trolling heads in their myriad forms, sizes and colours have proven their worth for trolling on the high seas and will take billfish, tuna, mackerel; most pelagic game fish in fact. Some have concave faces, others flat or convex, but they all function in the same way, albeit at different trolling speeds.

You know when they are at the right speed (usually about 8 knots but may be more or less), because you will see the lure pop up to the surface, take a gulp or bubble of air then submerge leaving a distinct bubble trail beneath the surface and that's it: It's the repetitive surface splash then ensuing bubble trail sequence that elicits the strike, and that goes for black lures, white lures and every conceivable colour in between.

While some lures, like bibbed and bibles minnows can be clipped directly onto your wind-on leader, I strongly suggest that when using skirted lures, which can run back up the leader or trace when a fish is hooked, that you rig it on a separate trace that can be clipped on. This is because a secondary strike on a lure that has been allowed to slide all the way back to the loop splice will usually cause a separation and that's something I've learned to my cost.

You will need a suitable size skirted trolling lure, both for the fish you are seeking and the tackle you are using. You will also need about a 6 foot (1.8 metre) length of trace line, once again about five times the test of your I.G.F.A. line class, a plastic bead from 0.2 to 0.3 inches (5 to 8 mm), and a length of line of about half the test of your trace with which to make a stopper knot. Use a strong, straight pattern hook of which there are many, but the Mustad 7691 in the appropriate size for the lure is a good choice.

I usually tie my lure traces in the same way that I described tying the swivel to the wind-on leader, but if you secure the hook with a crimp or swage then you will need a couple of those, making sure they are of the correct size for the trace line, and a crimping tool as you did for the wire. You will also need a short length of hard vinyl or plastic tubing, or armour spring, to protect the loop holding the hook from the wear and tear of trolling and bringing in fish.

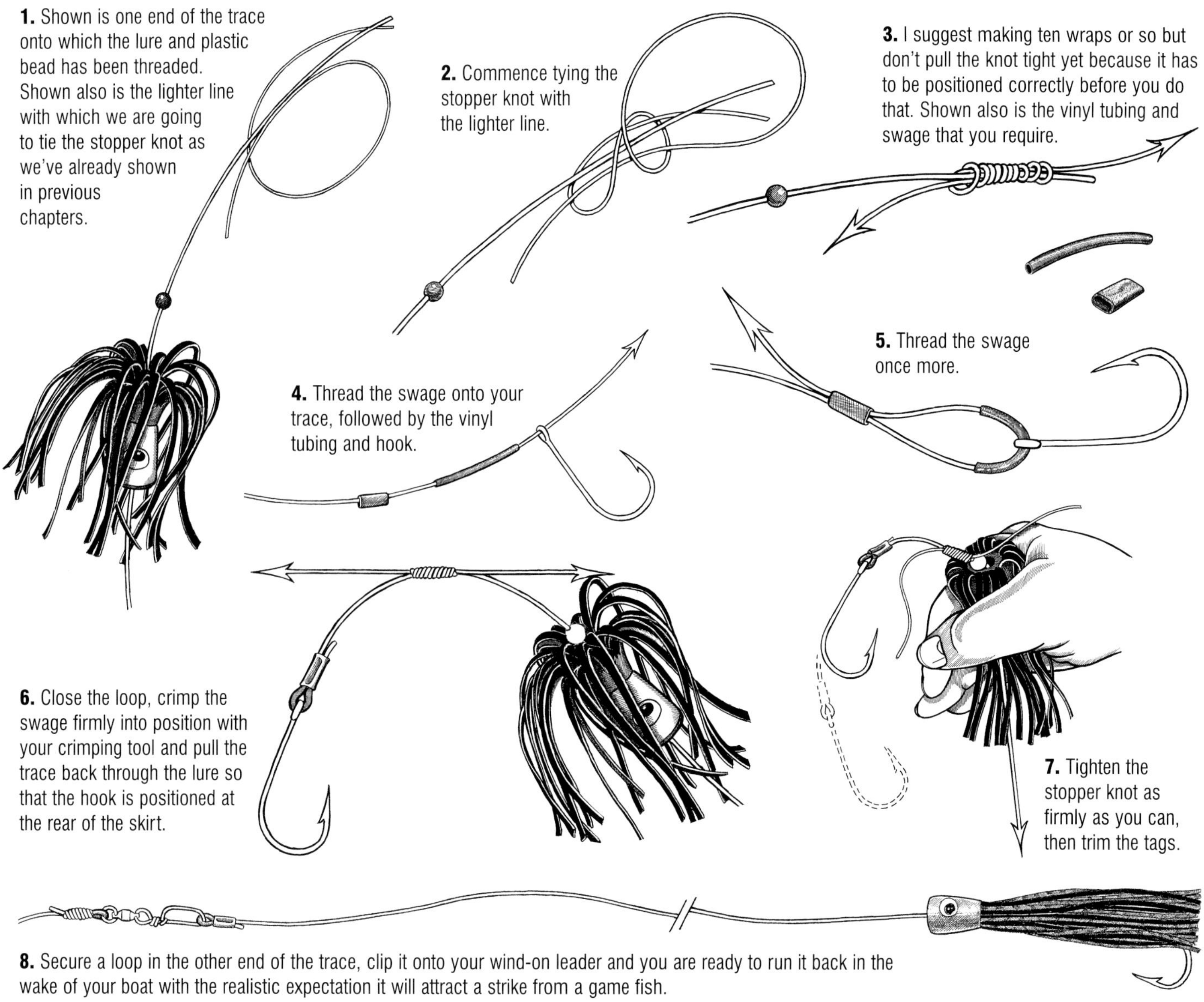

1. Shown is one end of the trace onto which the lure and plastic bead has been threaded. Shown also is the lighter line with which we are going to tie the stopper knot as we've already shown in previous chapters.

2. Commence tying the stopper knot with the lighter line.

3. I suggest making ten wraps or so but don't pull the knot tight yet because it has to be positioned correctly before you do that. Shown also is the vinyl tubing and swage that you require.

4. Thread the swage onto your trace, followed by the vinyl tubing and hook.

5. Thread the swage once more.

6. Close the loop, crimp the swage firmly into position with your crimping tool and pull the trace back through the lure so that the hook is positioned at the rear of the skirt.

7. Tighten the stopper knot as firmly as you can, then trim the tags.

8. Secure a loop in the other end of the trace, clip it onto your wind-on leader and you are ready to run it back in the wake of your boat with the realistic expectation it will attract a strike from a game fish.

Making a Single Strand Wire Trace

Single strand wire traces, in the appropriate gauge are useful for making traces for sport and game fish and for rigging fish baits for trolling. The original single strand wire used for this purpose was piano wire. Then came single strand high quality stainless steel wire followed by titanium single strand wire which is a further improvement.

However, while single strand wire traces are suitable for casting and trolling with bibbed and bibles lures, they are not suitable for trolling with skirted trolling heads, or any other type of lure that's designed to be threaded onto the trace.
This is because metal fatigue will eventually release the lure.

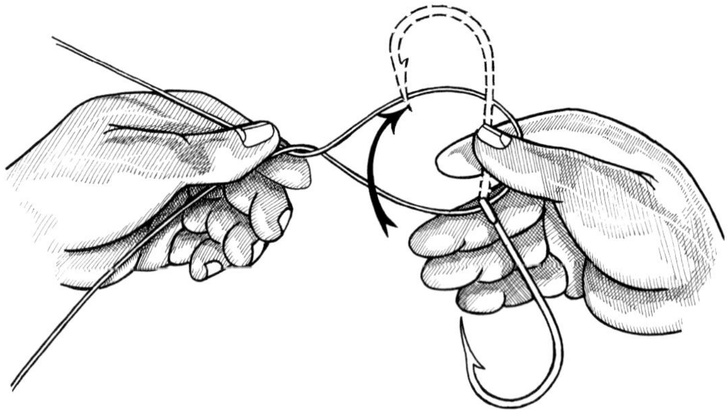

1. Thread the hook, swivel or lure onto the wire, isolate it on a loop and rotate the loop as shown. The most important thing here is that the wire be rotated to form nice evenly tensioned wraps.

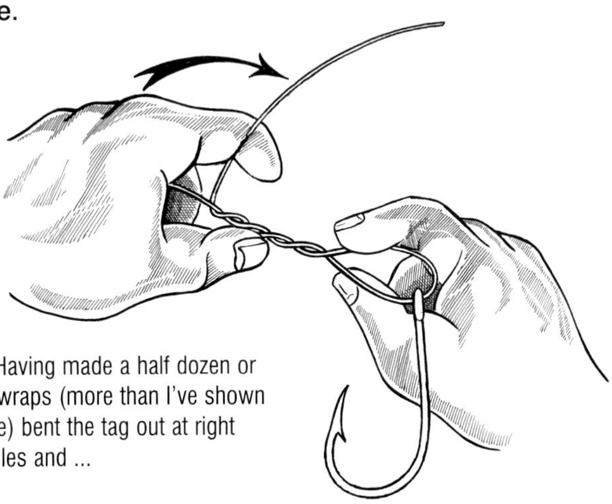

2. Having made a half dozen or so wraps (more than I've shown here) bent the tag out at right angles and ...

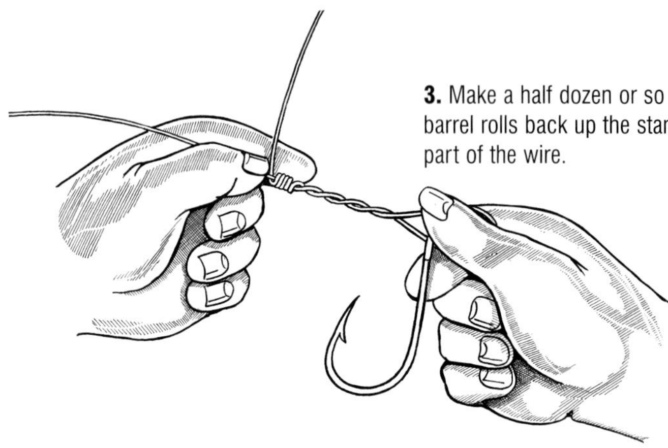

3. Make a half dozen or so tight barrel rolls back up the standing part of the wire.

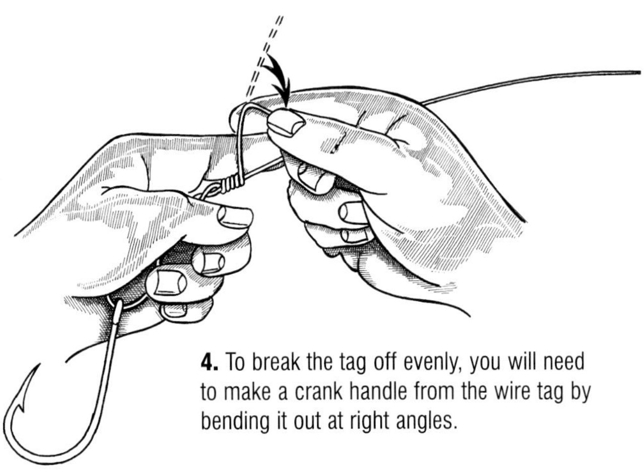

4. To break the tag off evenly, you will need to make a crank handle from the wire tag by bending it out at right angles.

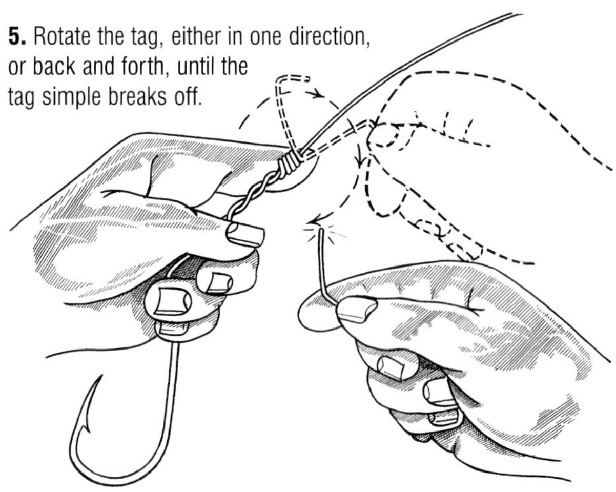

5. Rotate the tag, either in one direction, or back and forth, until the tag simple breaks off.

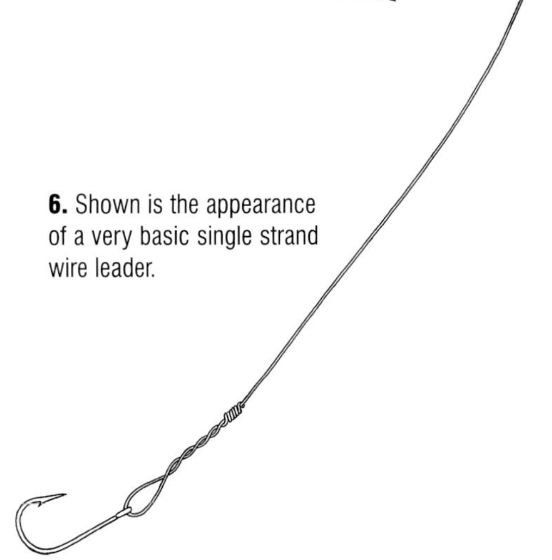

6. Shown is the appearance of a very basic single strand wire leader.

Du-Bro Wire Tools

While I can give instructions on making single strand wire leaders, I do recommend investigating the Du-Bro range of wire-tying tools http://www.dubro.com/ which make working with single strand wire a good deal easier that with your bare hands. The item I've illustrated here is the Du-Bro EZ twist that is specifically designed to make the haywire twist and barrel roll required to produce single strand wire leaders like the one described here.